FOREWORD

This Essential Knowledge Handbook has been produced for students of Edexcel GCSE 9-1 Business. It contains the essential theory required by the **Theme 2 specification** on **Building a Business**. It is ideal for independent learning, as well as to develop, clarify, consolidate and test students' knowledge and understanding of topics covered in class.

The author, **Claire Baker**, is an experienced teacher, examiner, author and the owner and Managing Director of **APT Initiatives Ltd** - a leading, quality provider of resources for Business and Economics. Having previously worked in industry, Claire has taught Business from ages 11 to 19 and has been an Examiner, Principal Examiner and Reviser for Business and Business related courses for a leading awarding body.

The book is divided into 5 main sections and 19 sub-sections, which match the topics and sub-topics of the Theme 2 Specification. At the beginning of each sub-section there is a summary of what students need to learn. These summaries, and the **explanations** that follow, take into account Edexcel's specification, content guidance, scheme of work and sample assessment material (published at the time of writing) - to ensure all examinable subject content is covered. Explanations are sufficiently detailed to enable students to grasp the essential theory required with minimum teacher assistance. **Key terms** are signposted throughout using the logo **KT**, and a **detailed index** is provided at the end of the Handbook - to enable students to quickly access the information they require.

'Essential Knowledge Checklists' are also provided at the end of each sub-section (sub-topic). These comprise a range of exam-style questions which students can work through and answer - using the in-depth explanations provided, or which teachers can set as homework, or as more formal tests in class. These essential knowledge questions largely use the command words 'define', 'give', 'calculate', 'explain' and 'discuss'. Based on Edexcel's sample assessment material (published at the time of writing), 'define' or 'give' questions are generally worth **1 mark**, 'calculate' questions are worth **2 marks**, 'explain' questions are worth **3 marks**, and 'discuss' questions are worth **6 marks**. 'Define' questions require students to define a term from the specification content. 'Give' questions require students to give an answer testing recall of knowledge from the specification content. 'Calculate' questions require students to use mathematical skills to reach an answer, based on given data (calculators may be used and working should be given). 'Explain' questions require students to give a statement of fact with two further expansion points (which may expand upon each other or upon the same fact). 'Discuss' questions require students to write an extended answer, requiring expansion and exploration of a business concept or issue. In these 6-mark questions, just 2 or 3 relevant, well-developed points should be sufficient to secure the maximum mark.

A range of activities to test and develop students' knowledge and understanding of the business studies theory and concepts covered in this Essential Knowledge Handbook is provided in other resources available from APT Initiatives Ltd. These include **7 Topic and End of Theme Test Papers** and **100 Multiple Choice Questions** (Interactive and / or Printable) for Theme 2 (and for Theme 1). **APT Initiatives Ltd** can be contacted directly with any orders, queries or feedback via the website: www.apt-initiatives.com, via email: support@apt-initiatives.com, or by phone: 01952 540877.

CONT

Topic 2.1 Growing the business

2.1.1 Business growth	2
2.1.2 Changes in business aims and objectives	17
2.1.3 Business and globalisation	22
2.1.4 Ethics, the environment and business	29

Topic 2.2 Making marketing decisions — **33**

2.2.1 Product	34
2.2.2 Price	41
2.2.3 Promotion	45
2.2.4 Place	52
2.2.5 Using the marketing mix to make business decisions	56

Topic 2.3 Making operational decisions — **61**

2.3.1 Business operations	62
2.3.2 Working with suppliers	71
2.3.3 Managing quality	80
2.3.4 The sales process	83

Topic 2.4 Making financial decisions — **86**

2.4.1 Business calculations	87
2.4.2 Understanding business performance	93

Topic 2.5 Making human resource decisions — **99**

2.5.1 Organisational structures	100
2.5.2 Effective recruitment	116
2.5.3 Effective training and development	122
2.5.4 Motivation	129

Topic 2.1

Growing the business

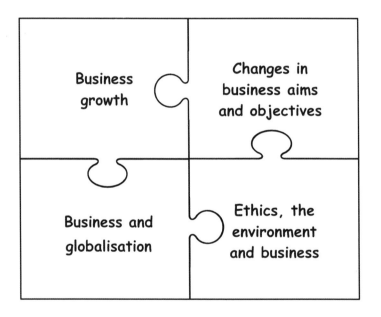

Business growth

Changes in business aims and objectives

Business and globalisation

Ethics, the environment and business

Business Growth (2.1.1)

What you need to learn

Methods of business growth and their impact:

➤ internal (organic) growth: new products (innovation, research and development), new markets (through changing the marketing mix or taking advantage of technology and / or expanding overseas); benefits and drawbacks.

➤ external (inorganic) growth: merger, takeover; benefits and drawbacks.

The types of business ownership for growing businesses:

➤ public limited company (plc).

Sources of finance for growing and established businesses:

➤ internal sources: retained profit, selling assets; advantages and limitations.

➤ external sources: loan capital, share capital, including stock market flotation (public limited companies); advantages and limitations.

Introduction - Benefits and Drawbacks of Growth in General

Growth is a key **business aim**. It generally brings **greater revenues** and **profits**, and leads to a business being **worth more**. In addition, it can **reduce unit costs** as a result of **economies of scale**. This will enable a business to be **more competitive on price** and / or **more profitable**. **KT Economies of scale** are factors that lead to a reduction in the unit (or average) cost as a business's output / size and scale of operations increases. For example, a larger business may be able to **buy in bulk** and **secure lower prices / discounts** from suppliers for doing so, thus reducing **unit material (variable) costs**. This is known as **KT purchasing** economies of scale.

Growth can, however, result in **KT diseconomies of scale**, that is, factors that cause **unit costs to rise** as a business increases its output / size and scale of operations. These concern the problems of managing large businesses - the fact that, as a business grows in size, **effective internal communication, coordination and control** become much more difficult. Diseconomies are more likely to result when **growth is rapid** and appropriate systems are unable to be developed in time to cope with growth.

Rapid growth can also result in a situation of **overtrading**. **KT Overtrading** is expansion without generating or organising sufficient cash in time to fund the expansion and meet debts as they fall due. Business growth should, therefore, be **carefully controlled** and backed up by **sufficient finance**. It should also take place at a **pace** that enables appropriate systems to be developed to aid **effective coordination and control** and, thereby, avoid **diseconomies** of scale.

Methods of business growth and their impact

Internal (organic) growth including benefits and drawbacks

Overview

KT **Internal growth**, also known as **organic growth**, does not involve buying (taking over) or joining together (merging) with another existing business. It often involves the use of **internal finance**, ie ploughing back profits, or asking existing shareholders to contribute more capital, in order to slowly build up assets, capacity and output, and expand the business's customer base - through **existing** or **new products** and **markets**.

The specification requires you to know and understand how internal growth can be achieved through **new products** and / or **new markets**. Before focusing on these ways of achieving growth, it should be appreciated that internal growth can also be achieved through **existing** products and / or markets.

Internal (organic) growth through existing products and markets

Internal (organic) growth through **existing** products and / or markets could be achieved by **changing elements of the marketing mix**. For example, a business may achieve sales growth organically by reducing price, improving product quality, improving customer service (through staff training) and / or increasing investment in promotion. It could also be achieved by **taking advantage of new technology**. For example:

- A **new 'state of the art' factory** may enable a business to **increase production volumes** and, thus, achieve **growth in sales and market share** (assuming there is increased demand for the business's products). At the same time, it may enable a business to **reduce costs** (eg labour, materials, energy, repairs and maintenance). This is because labour may be replaced by the new machinery, which tends to be more efficient and reliable. This would enable a business to be **more competitive on price**, which could help to achieve **growth in sales and market share** (and / or increased profits and, ultimately, the return to shareholders).

- **Social media technology** can also help a business to achieve growth through **existing** products and markets. This is because it provides the facility for businesses to very **quickly and cheaply interact** with **existing customers** (for instance using Instagram, Facebook, Twitter and Snapchat), and **remind them** of any **special offers or events**, and this can help to **increase sales**. It can also be a very cheap and highly cost effective way to reach potential **new customers**. This is because it enables existing customers to **instantly share information**, including word of mouth reviews about the business and its products / services - with friends, family and / or work colleagues, and this can help to **increase sales**.

Internal (organic) growth through new products

Achieving internal (organic) growth through **new products** involves **innovation** and often requires significant investment in **research and development**. **KT** **Innovation** is the successful implementation of a new idea which could, for example, concern a new product, process, approach or strategy. There are various **stages** involved, as follows:

1. Identification of new ideas.
2. Screening and selection of new ideas.
3. Detailed investigation into new ideas.
4. Pilot production / Production of a prototype.
5. Testing and review.
6. Full Launch.

One of the key activities associated with innovation is **research and development** R&D): **KT** **Research** is the study of a particular subject or market in order to further knowledge in this subject or market. **KT** **Development** is the application of this knowledge resulting in new products (or processes). In detail, R&D involves:

- carrying out research into new ideas / areas of interest.
- inventing, designing, testing and developing new ideas to meet customer and / or business needs and complying with legal requirements.
- assisting in the development of prototypes and / or the selection, installation, construction of equipment necessary to implement new products or processes.
- modifying existing products or processes in light of changing business / customer needs and / or competitor activities.
- gaining feedback on new (or modifications of existing) products or processes.

Innovation involves **significant costs**. In addition to the **cost of R&D**, there are costs associated with the **launch and implementation** of new products (or processes), such as **training,** as well as the cost of **promotional campaigns**.

Taking advantage of technology is listed in the specification as a means to achieve internal growth through **new markets**, but this can also be a means to achieve internal growth through **new products**. For example:

- Social media technology can be a **cheap** way to undertake **market research** to aid **new product development**. For instance, simply **searching the latest posts** and popular terms on social media platforms, such as Facebook and Twitter, can gain **real-time information on customer needs and preferences**, as well as **emerging trends and gaps** in the market.
- New technology may enable a business to produce products that they **were not able to produce before**, such as robotic lawnmowers and self-driving cars.
- Social media such as Instagram, Facebook, Twitter and Snapchat, can also be used to **showcase new products,** which can help to **maximise sales**.

© Claire Baker - APT Initiatives Ltd, 2018
© Claire Baker - APT Initiatives Ltd, 2018

Internal growth through new markets

Internal growth can be achieved by selling to **new markets**. This may involve a business in:

- targeting **new segments** - for example - different age groups, social and economic classes, industry or household, in **present geographical markets**, or
- targeting **new geographical markets** - nationally or overseas.

Targeting new markets generally requires significant **investment in promotion** in order to raise awareness of the product's existence in the new market.

Growth through new markets may be achieved quickly and relatively cheaply by **taking advantage of Internet technology**. For example, a business may sell its products / services via a **website** and having a website provides a business with access to a **global market**. It should, however, be appreciated that selling products to **overseas markets** might require **significant changes to elements of the marketing mix** - to cater for **different tastes** and / or **financial circumstances**.

Benefits of internal (organic) growth

The very first paragraph on this topic explained the benefits associated with growth in general, namely **growth in revenue** and **overall profit**, **reduction in costs** and, thus, **higher profits / profitability** as a result of **economies of scale**. Internal growth can also be **far less challenging and disruptive** than external (inorganic) growth through mergers and takeovers (discussed later below). This is because a business growing organically can **maintain the existing management and culture**. Therefore, there is **no scope for conflict** to arise from a clash of leadership styles / organisational cultures such as those that can occur with growth through mergers and takeovers.

In addition, internal (organic) growth is **not** likely to require **as much finance** as external (inorganic) growth through takeovers. This is because it does not involve the purchase of an existing business, brand name and customer goodwill, which often involves paying shareholders a price for their shares which is above the market price.

Drawbacks of internal (organic) growth

One of the drawbacks of internal (organic) growth, relative to external (inorganic) growth, is that it is often **slower**, especially if funds are limited to **internal** sources. This is because, with organic growth, the business is not buying an existing business with existing facilities and workforce trained and experienced in meeting the needs of an established customer base, and building a customer base can take years. As a consequence, a strategy of internal growth might mean a business **loses out on sales and market share** to businesses pursuing a strategy of external growth.

External (inorganic) growth including benefits and drawbacks

Overview

KT **External growth**, also known as **inorganic growth**, involves a business **buying or joining together with another business**. It consists of **mergers** and **acquisitions**, which includes **takeovers** (defined later below). It involves a firm acquiring additional resources from (or with) other businesses. These resources may include:

- **KT** **Tangible assets**. These are items that a business owns that can be seen or touched. They include land, buildings, fixtures and fittings, machinery and vehicles. A business's workforce could also be classed as a tangible asset.

- **KT** **Intangible assets**. These are items that a business owns that cannot be seen or touched. They include goodwill, patents, copyrights and trademarks including brand names and website domain names. Note: **KT** **Goodwill** is the estimated value placed on regular custom established over the years. It usually only appears when one business takes over another, and is usually the difference between the Net Asset Value and the purchase price of the company.

Mergers

There are many definitions of mergers and takeovers, which can lead to confusion. In GCSE Business, **KT** **mergers** are generally defined as taking place when two or more existing businesses agree to join together to form a new business and cease to be distinct enterprises, rather than remaining separately owned and operated. This typically involves two relatively equal, similar sized businesses joining together, under a common board of directors. Most mergers involve the newly combined business taking on a new identity and being given a new name, which often incorporates the names (or part of the names) of the original businesses. The shareholders of the combining businesses mutually share the risks and rewards of the new business, and no one party to the merger obtains control over the other.

In practice, 'mergers of equals' do not happen very often; usually one company buys another, which may take place with or without the agreement of the directors of the business being taken over.

Takeovers

KT A **takeover** is where one company (the 'acquirer' or 'bidder' or 'predator') buys a majority stake (51%) in another company (the target), and thus gains control of the company. This is often called an **acquisition,** but acquisitions may not always involve a business buying a controlling stake in another business; they may more simply involve a business buying one or more parts (eg sites) of another business.

When a takeover takes place, the acquired company becomes either a **subsidiary** of the acquiring company or, alternatively (which is often the case), is **absorbed into** the operations of the acquiring company. The acquiring company is usually much larger than the target (acquired) company.

People often regard takeovers as being *'hostile'*, that is, against the wishes of the target company's board of directors, shareholders and management. Some takeovers are, however, welcomed by the key stakeholders of the company that is taken over. Therefore, a distinction should be made between a **welcome** or **'friendly'** takeover, and an **unwelcome** or **'hostile'** takeover.

Benefits of mergers and takeovers

A business can grow **much more quickly** through mergers and takeovers than through internal (organic) growth. With mergers and takeovers a business may benefit from:

- **immediate increased revenues** and, thus, **overall profit** from the new business, as long as the additional revenue is greater than any additional costs incurred.

- a **reduction in overheads** - as a result of eliminating **duplicate** positions / departments. For instance, if two firms merge, there will be no need for two Chief Executives or two HR or PR departments.

- a significant **reduction in unit (average) costs** as a result of **economies of scale**. This is most likely to be the case when the two businesses are at the same stage in the supply chain and have the same target market(s). As highlighted previously, with **lower unit costs**, a business can **lower prices** - to win sales from competitors and / or encourage customers to buy more. This could **increase overall revenue** and **market share**. Alternatively, with lower unit costs, a business can enjoy **higher profits**. This would provide **greater funds for reinvestment** and / or **higher dividends to shareholders**.

Drawbacks of mergers and takeovers

There are a number of **costs** associated with mergers and takeovers. These include:

- the **cost of integrating** the new business(es).
- the cost of any **redundancies** - in terms of redundancy payments (as a result of eliminating duplicate positions / departments, for example).
- the **original purchase cost** - if it involves a **takeover**.

Any talk of takeover or merger produces **uncertainty and anxiety** amongst employees. Employees might become worried about the security of their jobs and possible changes that may be made following the takeover or merger. These feelings of uncertainty can be **disruptive** and, in extreme cases, can result in **poor motivation** and, as a result, **poor performance** - for example - in terms of **productivity** and / or **quality**.

In situations of takeover and merger, there can be **major cultural differences** between the two businesses, especially when it involves the takeover of a business overseas, resulting in **conflict** and **poor post-merger / takeover performance**. For instance, one board of directors - in the case of a merger, or senior managers and individual managers - in the case of a takeover, might have a different philosophy on **leadership style**, **ethics** and **strategy**. Different ideas regarding the treatment of staff could also lead to employees feeling **uncertain** and **insecure**.

There is also a possible **threat to customer retention** following a merger or takeover - if customers perceive that the new owner (following a takeover) has made unnecessary changes and feel the product is not the same since 'they' took over. There are, in fact, many consumers who felt that the taste of *Cadbury's* chocolate changed for the worse following the *Kraft* takeover (in 2010). This could have negatively affected sales. In addition, when two companies with major brand names join together, there might be **confusion in brand values**. This could also threaten customer retention.

Not surprisingly, the performance of firms during the first year after a takeover may be disappointing. Whether or not the problems described above arise, will largely depend on **whether the acquired firm is to be run as a separate business or not**. If the acquired firm is to become part of the acquiring firm, then redundancies and problems with overcoming cultural differences are **more likely** to be encountered.

The types of business ownership for growing businesses

Public limited company (plc)

Definition and key characteristics

KT A **public limited company (plc)** is a business that is owned by **two or more individuals or companies** (known as shareholders) and which acquires **a separate legal identity** to its owners. This means that the business can own property, sue and be sued and that the business's finances are separate to the owners (shareholders). This is the same for private limited companies (Ltd's) and limited liability partnerships, which were covered in Theme 1, although Ltd's can be owned by just **one** individual (as opposed to two).

Like Ltd's, with plc's:

- The **liability** of the owners (ie shareholders) for business debts is **limited** to what the owners have paid (or what they have agreed to pay) for their shares.

- **Finance** comes from the **sale of shares** in the business (and may also come from loans and retained profits). In a plc, however, shares are bought and sold by **members of the general public on the stock exchange** (discussed further later).

Unlike Ltd's, with plc's:

- Shareholders elect / appoint at least **two directors** (as opposed to just one) to make all the key business decisions and manage the business on their behalf.

- A plc must also appoint a formally **qualified Company Secretary** who, along with directors, is responsible for submitting key legal documents to Companies House.

- Once a plc has been issued with a **Certificate of Incorporation** it must carry out **a number of additional procedures**, before it can start trading. It is also subject to **more ongoing rules and regulations**. These are outlined under disadvantages below.

Advantages / Benefits

- Like Ltd's, the **liability** of the owners (shareholders) for settling business debts is **limited** to what they have paid or what they have agreed to pay for their shares. This means that, in the event a business is unable to pay its bills and the business's assets are insufficient to settle all debts, the finances and personal assets of the owners (shareholders) are protected beyond what they have invested in shares.

- Like Ltd's, plc's have **greater continuity** than sole traders or partnerships. This is because the business is not dissolved upon the resignation, bankruptcy or death of a shareholder (owner) or director, as shares can simply be transferred to another / other owners.

- Plc's have **greater capital raising opportunities** than other types of business ownership. This is because finance can be raised through selling shares to members of the public on the Stock Exchange. Note: KT The **stock exchange** is a market in which securities eg stocks (shares), bonds, debentures, and any other ownership investments, are bought and sold.

- Plc status may provide **enhanced prestige** and a **more professional image** than other types of business, such as sole traders. This can make it easier to secure customers.

- A plc is also generally **more widely known** - due to the fact that shares are advertised for sale to the public. This may also make it easier to secure customers.

Disadvantages / Drawbacks

Plc's are **more complex** and, therefore, **more time consuming to set up** than other types of business ownership, including Ltd's. This is because, in order to become a public limited company, not only does the business have to submit a memorandum of association, articles of association and a Form 10 and Form 12, plc's must also undertake the following before the business can start trading (as a plc):

1. **Produce a prospectus** detailing company history and prospects, and inviting members of the public to buy shares in the business.
2. **Issue shares** to the value of **at least £50,000** – of which a quarter must be paid.
3. Await the receipt of a **Trading Certificate** from Companies House.
4. Appoint **at least two directors and** a **Company Secretary** whose conduct and duties are governed by law.

Plc's are, therefore, **more expensive to set up** than other types of business ownership, including Ltd's. This is because, in addition to the administration fee they have to pay to register as a limited company, floating a company on the stock exchange can be a very expensive (and time consuming) process. The issue of **a prospectus** promoting the company to potential shareholders is one of the **major costs**. The prospectus will actually form part of the contract between the business and its shareholders and so, in addition to **printing and marketing costs**, **legal fees** are likely to be incurred from the employment of a solicitor to check through the prospectus. **Underwriters** also have to be found as a requirement of the Stock Exchange, to purchase any unsold shares, and underwriters **charge a fee**.

Plc's are subject to far **more government regulations** than any other type of business. These concern the submission of accounts and qualifications and conduct of directors / company officials, as well as information provided to shareholders. For example, like Ltd's, they have to file separate accounts. However, unlike Ltd's, these accounts must be **audited**, a **fully qualified Company Secretary** must be appointed, and an **Annual General Meeting** (AGM) must be held for shareholders. As a result of all the government regulations a plc has to follow, a plc might develop **many procedures** and, thus, be **slower to react to change**.

Plc's also have **more ongoing costs** than sole traders and ordinary partnerships, as well as than Ltd's. Like Ltd's, having to file separate accounts incurs accountancy fees, and having to file a confirmation statement each year (confirming key company details) with Companies House, incurs an annual fee. In addition, the fact that plc's must employ a fully qualified Company Secretary and also have their accounts audited, increases **labour costs** and incurs **auditing fees**.

For a plc there is also the **threat of takeover**, that is, the chance of an individual or other business organisation obtaining more than 50% of the shares. This is because shares can be bought and sold on the stock exchange by members of the general public.

Another disadvantage associated with becoming a plc concerns **divorce of ownership and control**. Selling shares in the business to **members of the public** means that more people (shareholders) obtain the right to vote on important matters, such as the election of directors and key decisions relating to the strategic direction of the business. As more and more people become involved in a business, the **potential for conflict** - between the original owner-director(s) and shareholders - is greater.

© Claire Baker - APT Initiatives Ltd, 2018
© Claire Baker - APT Initiatives Ltd, 2018

Shareholders are also entitled to a **share in the profits**, although it is up to the directors to decide how much of the profits will be paid to the shareholders and how much will be reinvested each year.

Like Ltd's, plc's are **less flexible** than sole traders and ordinary and limited partnerships. This is because they are restricted to the objects of the business listed in registration documents (although these can be changed through a formal written procedure and agreement between the owners).

Like Ltd's, the company's **financial affairs do not remain private** (unlike sole traders and ordinary and limited partnerships). This is because the Annual Accounts and Reports they have to file with Companies House can be viewed by members of the public.

Sources of finance for growing and established businesses

Introduction

KT *Method* of finance is *how* the finance is raised. **KT** *Source* of finance is from *where* the finance is obtained. In practice, the distinction between these two terms has become blurred and when students are asked to comment on sources, answers relating to methods are generally what is required.

There are several sources (methods) of finance to be covered in Theme 2, which have already been examined in Theme 1, namely retained profit, loans and share capital. These are explained again below, together with the additional sources (methods) of selling assets and selling shares specifically through a stock market flotation.

Internal sources (including advantages and disadvantages / limitations)

Overview

KT **Internal sources of finance** are generated from **within** the business. These include:

- **profit** which is **retained** after all costs, taxes and dividends (if any) have been deducted from revenues.
- **the sale of business assets** (such as land, buildings, vehicles and machinery) that are no longer needed, or do not make enough contribution to the firm's profits.

Retained profit

KT **Retained profit** is the money remaining after cost of sales, other expenses, interest, tax and any dividends to shareholders have been deducted from revenue. It is profit which is reinvested in the business.

Advantages:

- Using retained profit is a **quick and easy** source of finance. This is because profit is available immediately, and there is no need, for example, to publicise assets for sale (as with selling assets), or publicise shares for sale (as with selling shares) or fill in any application forms (as with securing a bank loan).

- It is an **inexpensive** source of finance. In contrast to loan capital, it does not incur interest payments. Neither does it incur any company registration or legal fees, such as those associated with selling shares in the business.

- It is the **least risky** source of finance. Unlike bank loans, for example, there is no need to provide any guarantees or security, that is, collateral in the form of fixed assets that the bank can seize if loan repayments are not met.

- It **does not dilute ownership and control** - as with selling shares (or further dilute ownership and control - if the business is already set up as a limited company and decides to sell more shares). This means that key business decisions can be taken without the interference of shareholders, and the business profits do not have to be shared (distributed) amongst shareholders.

Disadvantages / Limitations:

- For an established business set up as a private limited company, using retained profit **might not be popular with shareholders**. This is because shareholders receive a dividend (a percentage of a business's after tax annual profit), and use of retained profit could mean low or even no dividend payments for at least a year.

- Sole reliance on profits could mean that **expansion is slow** - if profits are not particularly high, and so a business might lose out on increasing sales and market share (in relation to competitors).

Selling assets

KT **Assets** are items owned by a business. **KT** **Selling assets** is the selling of items owned by a business, typically **non-current (fixed) assets**, that are no longer used or are not considered to be making enough contribution to the business's profits. **KT** **Non-current assets** (or **fixed assets**) may be **tangible** such as buildings, **non-tangible** such as trademarks and / or **financial** such as shares in other businesses.

Advantages:

- Selling business assets is likely to be a **less costly** way of raising finance than loans or selling shares through a stock market flotation. This is because there are no interest payments - as with bank loans. In addition, advertising assets for sale is likely to be much cheaper than a stock market flotation, which involves underwriting fees, fees to solicitors / advisers, printing a prospectus, as well as advertising shares for sale.

- Selling assets **does not dilute ownership and control** as with selling shares. This means that key business decisions can be made without the interference of shareholders and, thus, decisions can be made more quickly. It also means that the business profits do not have to be shared (distributed) amongst any new owners (ie shareholders).

Disadvantages / Limitations:

- It can be **difficult to sell property quickly.** Therefore, if funds were required quickly, then a business might be forced to sell **at a lower price** than that which could have been realised in the longer term.

- Selling assets could **restrict the business's future flexibility.** A business should be certain that the asset is no longer needed in the business. If it is, then it might be possible to sell the asset and **lease** it back. This would provide the finance required for investment, as well as continued use of the asset. **KT Leasing** is an external method of finance for a start-up or an established business. It is where a business rents a non-current (fixed) asset rather than purchasing it outright and where the ownership of the asset remains with the leasing company.

External sources (including advantages and disadvantages / limitations)

Overview

KT External sources of finance come from **outside** the business. These include trade credit, debt factoring, leasing and hire purchase, overdrafts, loans (including mortgages) and debentures, share capital, venture capital and government grants. Those required to be covered for Theme 2, (which were also required for Theme 1), concern **loan capital** and **share capital**.

Loan capital

KT Loan capital is money borrowed from individuals or organisations which must be repaid within a specified period, at an agreed rate of interest.

Example: If a growing business borrowed £100,000 to fund its planned expansion, at a fixed annual rate of 6% for a period of 3 years, it would pay annual interest of £100,000 x 0.06 = £6,000. This would amount to £6,000 x 3 = £19,000 over 3 years.

Note: The interest rate may be fixed or variable, although many lenders provide the opportunity of switching from one to the other at pre-specified periods.

Loans may be obtained from a **bank** or other finance company in the form of a short, medium or long-term loan, or from individual members of the public in the form of **debentures.**

KT Debentures are a type of loan, where the money to be raised is divided into smaller units, and members of the public are invited to lend money to the business for a fixed period of time, usually long term, and at a fixed rate of interest. They are bought and sold on the Stock Exchange. Those companies successful in raising money this way are usually well established, have a good profit record and a sound liquidity (cash flow) position. New or young companies would find it difficult to secure the public's confidence.

Advantages:

- Loans are **relatively straightforward to arrange,** providing the business is **solvent** (ie it can pay its debts) and has a satisfactory financial history.

- Loans are **generally cheaper than overdrafts** - as interest rates tend to be lower.

- Unlike overdrafts, there is **no danger of the loan being recalled** before the agreed date to repay the loan expires (unless the loan conditions are breached).

- It **does not dilute ownership and control** - as with share capital (and venture capital). This means key business decisions can be taken without the interference of shareholders, and the business profits do not have to be shared (distributed) amongst shareholders.

Disadvantages / Limitations:

- A business has to pay **interest** on the loan taken out (in addition to repaying the loan after the agreed period of time). This **increases costs,** which has implications for cash-flow and **reduces profit.** Unlike dividends with shareholders, the interest must be paid even if the firm is not making a profit.

- Interest rates might also **rise** during the period of the loan. This would **increase the cost** of taking out the loan (if the loan has a **variable** rate as opposed to **fixed** rate of interest).

- A loan usually requires **security (collateral)** in the form of **fixed assets** (such as land, buildings, equipment and vehicles), which the bank (or other lender) can claim if interest payments or loan repayments are not met.

- Loans tend to be **less flexible** and **less convenient than overdrafts.** This is because repayments are fixed and must be made on agreed dates.

Share capital, including stock market flotation (public limited companies)

Remember, from Theme 1, **KT share capital** is finance raised by selling a portion of the business - to family and friends in the case of private limited companies, or to members of the general public in the case of public limited companies, through a stock market flotation.

KT A **stock market flotation** (going 'public') is the process of converting a private limited company into a public limited company by issuing shares and inviting **the public** (individuals or other businesses) to purchase them.

Advantages of selling shares in general:

- There are **no commitments to meeting fixed payments** to the providers of the finance (ie shareholders), unlike the interest payable on loans from a bank, for example. This is because dividend payments (for ordinary shareholders at least) are not fixed and do not have to be paid in an unprofitable year.

Disadvantages / Limitations of selling shares in general:

- Selling shares **dilutes ownership, control** and **profits** of the business This is because, in return for their investment, shareholders (ie 'ordinary' shareholders as opposed to 'preference' shareholders) receive voting rights on important matters, such as the election of directors, as well as a variable **KT** **dividend** (a percentage of after-tax profits) according to how well the company has performed.

Advantages of a stock market flotation:

- The business will become **more widely known** - as shares are advertised for sale to the public. This may make it easier to secure customers, and thus to increase sales.

Disadvantages / Limitations of a stock market flotation:

- The process of share issue, especially one that involves a stock market flotation, can be **very expensive.** Costs include: underwriting fees, fees to solicitors / advisers, printing a company prospectus, and advertising shares for sale. Therefore, it is not worthwhile unless large sums are involved.

- The process of raising finance through a stock market flotation can be **time consuming** and **take several months longer** than other ways of raising finance; it takes an average of three to six months, but can take more than one year. It can, in fact, occupy a great deal of management time and, ultimately, take management focus away from the core activities of the business. Unless carefully planned, this could lead to a temporary drop in the performance of the business.

- Selling shares through a stock market flotation **increases the risk of a takeover** - by an individual or another business obtaining more than 50% of the shares. This is because, once a business is listed on a stock market, shares can easily be transferred from one person or business to another.

- As highlighted above, becoming a public limited company will also require the business to **comply with ongoing, additional regulatory requirements**. These concern the submission of company accounts, the qualifications and conduct of directors and other company officials, as well as information provided to shareholders. All these requirements will **incur additional ongoing costs**.

Essential Knowledge Checklist

*Questions you should now be able to answer on **business growth**:*

1. Define the following terms: a) internal (organic) growth b) innovation c) research and development d) external (inorganic) growth e) merger f) takeover g) public limited company h) the stock exchange i) internal sources of finance j) retained profit k) assets l) non-current (fixed) assets m) external sources of finance n) loan capital o) debentures p) share capital q) stock market flotation.

2. You should also be able to define the following terms: a) economies of scale b) tangible assets c) intangible assets d) goodwill e) leasing.

3. Explain **one** impact on a business (or **one** benefit or **one** drawback for a business) of: a) internal (organic) growth; b) external (inorganic) growth (mergers or takeovers).

4. Discuss the potential benefits for a business of each of the following: a) growing internally (organically); b) growing externally (inorganically).

5. Discuss the potential drawbacks for a business of each of the following: a) growing internally (organically); b) growing externally (inorganically).

6. Explain **one** reason why a private limited company (Ltd) might become a public limited company (plc) / Explain **one** advantage of becoming a public limited company.

7. Explain **one** disadvantage for a business of becoming a public limited company.

8. Discuss the potential benefits for a business of becoming a public limited company.

9. Discuss potential drawbacks for a business of becoming a public limited company.

10. Give **one** internal method of finance a growing and established business might use.

11. Give **one** external method of finance a growing and established business might use.

12. Explain **one** advantage for a business of using each of the following methods of finance: a) retained profit b) selling assets c) loan capital d) share capital, including a stock market flotation.

13. Explain **one** disadvantage or limitation for a business of using each of the following methods of finance: a) retained profit b) selling assets c) loan capital d) share capital, including a stock market flotation.

14. Explain **one** advantage for a business of using each of the following internal sources of finance over external sources of finance: a) retained profit b) selling assets.

15. Discuss the advantages for a business of using each of the following methods of finance: a) retained profit b) selling assets c) loan capital d) share capital, including a stock market flotation.

16. Discuss the disadvantages or limitations for a business of using each of the following methods of finance: a) retained profit b) selling assets c) loan capital d) share capital, including a stock market flotation.

17. Justify the most appropriate method of finance a growing or established business should use in a given situation.

© Claire Baker - APT Initiatives Ltd, 2018

© Claire Baker - APT Initiatives Ltd, 2018

Changes in Business Aims and Objectives (2.1.2)

What you need to learn

Why business aims and objectives change as businesses evolve:

➢ in response to: market conditions, technology, performance, legislation, internal reasons.

How business aims and objectives change as businesses evolve:

➢ focus on survival or growth
➢ entering or exiting markets
➢ growing or reducing the workforce
➢ increasing or decreasing product range.

Introduction

Remember, from Theme 1, **KT** **business aims and objectives** are goals or targets that businesses strive to achieve. **KT** **Aims** are broad statements of intent, usually expressed in vague terms, with no timescale, or precise target that can easily be measured. **KT** **Objectives** should be far more specific and clearly state what needs to be done in order to achieve the business's aims.

Why and how business aims and objectives change as businesses evolve

Reasons why business aims and objectives change

Introduction

Business aims and objectives may change as a business evolves as a result of changes in **external factors** and / or **internal factors**.

Changes in external factors

KT **External factors** are factors stemming from outside the business (factors over which a business has little or no control), which can affect decisions over, and / or the successful achievement of, the business's aims and objectives. These include changes in **market conditions**, **technology**, **legislation** and **the economic climate**. Note: The economic climate is not listed in the specification on this topic, but it can have a significant influence on business aims and objectives, as will be explained.

Internal reasons

Internal reasons that can affect decisions over (or success in achieving) business aims and objectives, include changes in:

- the business's **financial position**, eg changes in the level of profit a business makes (which may be influenced by external factors and / or other internal factors).
- the **size, quality and motivation of** a business's **workforce.**
- the **age** of the business / how long the business has been in existence.
- the **ownership** and / or **management** of the business.

Note: The specification lists '**performance**' as a reason why business aims and objectives change. This is listed separately to 'internal reasons' but could be classed as an internal reason, although it is influenced by external and internal factors.

How business aims and objectives change

Overview

Changes in external and internal factors could result in a business:

- **focusing on survival or growth**.
- **entering or exiting markets**.
- **growing or reducing the workforce**.
- **increasing or decreasing product range**.

Numerous examples are provided in the sub-sections that follow.

How business aims and objectives change in response to market conditions

Remember, from Theme 1, **KT** a **market** is a place where buyers and sellers get together to exchange products and services (for money). **KT** **Market conditions** are characteristics of a market such as the level of competition and rate of market growth, that is, growth in the sales of (and demand for) a particular product or service.

If the **market (demand)** for a business's product / service is **growing**, then a business might focus on **growth** in sales and profit, instead of just **surviving**. For instance:

- People are more **health conscious**, enabling businesses operating in these markets to set more ambitious **growth** objectives and / or providing opportunities for businesses operating in these markets to **increase their product range**.

- An **ageing population** is increasing the demand for certain types of holidays, medicines and household equipment, thus enabling businesses in these markets to set objectives relating to **growth** in customer numbers and sales.

If the **market (demand)** for a business's product or service is **declining**, then a business might decide to focus on **survival**, financial security (liquidity) and cost minimisation, instead of **growth** in sales and profit. It might also decide to **exit the (declining) market** and **enter new growth markets**.

A **new competitor** may also result in **reduced demand** for a business's product / service, and this might result in a business focusing on **maintaining** as opposed to **increasing** sales, market share and / or profit.

How business aims and objectives change in response to technology

Remember, from Theme 1, **KT** technology is the combination of skills, knowledge, tools, equipment, machines and computers used to undertake tasks. Advances in technology can result in business aims and objective changing in response. For example:

- New technology can lead to a **decline in the demand** for a business's products. For instance, film DVDs and music CDs are increasingly being replaced by downloads. This might force businesses operating in such markets to focus on **survival** (and cost minimisation) instead of **growth** (eg in sales and profit).

- Advances in technology can result in once popular products becoming **obsolete**. This might force a business to **exit existing (declining) markets** and enter **other related (growth) markets**. For instance, a business that supplied film DVDs or music CDs may be able to exploit its existing expertise and invest successfully in a website with e-commerce facilities to provide **downloadable versions** of these products.

- New technology may come in the form of new **cost saving machinery / equipment**. This may enable a business to focus on **growth in profit** - due to lower costs, and / or **growth in sales and market share** - if it lowers prices to its customers (as a result of lower costs).

- Advances in technology enable businesses to invest in **labour saving devices** - for example - automated machinery, computers, robots, and so reduce the number of people required to produce a business's products / provide a business's service, resulting in a business **reducing** rather than **increasing the size of its workforce**.

How business aims and objectives change in response to legislation

Remember, from Theme 1, **KT** legislation is the collection of laws which exist to protect employees, consumers and other stakeholders from being exploited by a business, and the potential negative effects that can arise as a result of business activity, such as pollution.

New legislation may necessitate **costly changes** in order to comply with the legislation, and this might force a business to revise its objectives relating to **profit**.

How business aims and objectives change in response to the economic climate

Remember, from Theme 1, **KT** the **economic climate** concerns the general condition or state of the economy and concerns changes in GDP, unemployment, levels of consumer income, inflation, interest rates, government taxation and exchange rates.

In a **recession** (two successive quarters of negative change in GDP), previous objectives relating to **growth** in sales and profit may be **unrealistic** and so a business may be forced to concentrate on **survival** - at least in the short term, and on **reducing the size of the workforce** - in order to **cut costs**.

A decrease in levels of **consumer income** may reduce the **demand** for consumer goods and, thus, force businesses providing such goods to focus on **survival** instead of **growth**. This may be as a result of an increase in **income tax, unemployment**, or **interest rates**.

An increase in **unemployment** will reduce the number of people who are able and willing to buy a business's product or service. This is because unemployed people have less income to spend on goods and services. This may force a business to focus on **survival** as opposed to **growth**, especially businesses selling luxuries (such as computer games and holidays) or income-sensitive goods (such as houses and cars), as opposed to necessities (such as food and medicines).

An increase in **interest rates** can reduce the demand for a business's products / service, which can force a business to revise its objectives relating to sales **growth**. This is because people with mortgages have less discretionary income to spend on goods and services, borrowing is more expensive which puts people off using credit to pay for goods and services, and consumers are also more likely to save rather than spend - as there is more reward for saving.

An increase in **interest rates** may also increase a business's **costs** - if it has borrowed money in the form a mortgage, loan or overdraft for example, and thus force a business to revise its objectives relating to **profit**.

Inflation also increases the **costs** a business has to pay for its resource inputs, that is, the materials used to make its products and / or the cost of labour required to provide its service. This may force a business to revise its objectives relating to **profit**.

How business aims and objectives change as a result of internal reasons

Business aims and objectives may change according to **how long the business has been in operation**. For example:

- Many businesses **just starting up** may be **content to survive and break-even** in the short to medium term. This may be due to a lack of experience, expertise and resources, or limited awareness and understanding of customer needs, or competition from established firms, or unexpected costs.

© Claire Baker - APT Initiatives Ltd, 2018

- As a business becomes **more established** and, as a result, more experienced and widely known, its objectives are likely to focus more on making a **profit** rather than just **surviving** and breaking even.

Growth in the size of the business can also lead to a change in business aims and objectives. This is because as a business grows in size, it may be able to adopt more ambitious **growth** objectives than smaller businesses due, for example, to having more assets to offer as security in order to raise loan capital to finance expansion.

The **performance** of a business will also lead to changes in a business's aims and objectives. For example, a healthy financial situation in terms of the **level of profit** being generated provides funds for investment, and this enables a business to focus on more ambitious **growth** objectives.

A **change in business ownership or management** can also lead to changes in a business's aims and objectives. For example:

- If the director(s) of a private limited company (Ltd) decided to form a public limited company (plc), they would be able to **raise more capital** to fund expansion - as finance can be raised by selling shares to the public. Therefore, the plc may have more ambitious objectives (**growth** in sales and market share) than the Ltd.

- Some business owners may be more willing to take a **risk** and, as a result, may pursue more ambitious **growth** objectives, such as diversification into new markets.

- New directors or managers may prefer to adopt different aims and objectives, or have different ideas on how such goals can, or should, be achieved.

Essential Knowledge Checklist

*Questions you should now be able to answer on **changes in business aims & objectives**:*

1. Define the term business aims and objectives.
2. You should also be able to define the following: a) external factors b) market conditions c) technology d) legislation e) the economic climate.
3. Explain **one** reason why business aims and objectives may change as a business evolves.
4. Explain **one external** reason why business aims and objectives may change as a business evolves.
5. Explain **one internal** reason why business aims and objectives may change as a business evolves.
6. Explain **one** way in which a business's aims and objectives may change in response to each of the following: market conditions, technology, legislation, economic climate.
7. Discuss how changes in each of the following may impact on a business's aims and objectives: a) market conditions b) technology c) legislation d) the economic climate.

Business and Globalisation (2.1.3)

What you need to learn

The impact of globalisation on businesses:

- imports: competition from overseas, buying from overseas (and the effect of changes in exchange rates)
- exports: selling to overseas markets (and the effect of changes in exchange rates)
- changing business locations - opportunities to relocate to low-cost locations overseas
- multinationals.

Barriers to international trade:

- tariffs
- trade blocs
- the effect these may have on businesses in restricting opportunities, efficiency ad competition.

How businesses compete internationally:

- the use of the Internet and e-commerce (to sell beyond national boundaries)
- changing the marketing mix to compete internationally (eg for different cultures, languages and regions).

Introduction

KT **Globalisation** can be defined as the process that has resulted in ever-closer links between the world's economies resulting in greater interdependence. It is evident, in particular, in the rise in:

- **global trade** - trade *between* countries as distinct from trade *within* individual countries.
- **Foreign Direct Investment (FDI)** - investment by foreign companies in productive capacity.
- **migration of workers** - the movement of workers from one country or region to another (ie across international boundaries).

The **growth in world trade** owes much to **the reduction in trade barriers**, which includes the reduction in and elimination of **tariffs** (and quotas), and the formation of **trade blocs**. It has forced businesses to consider **how to compete internationally**.

The impact of globalisation on businesses

Imports (and the impact of exchange rates)

Globalisation has led to **increased competition** for businesses from **imports**. KT An **import** is a good (or service) brought into a country from another country. This has put pressure on businesses to **cut costs** in order to **reduce prices,** and thereby remain competitive and, ultimately, **retain customers / maintain sales.**

On the other hand, globalisation has enabled businesses to **purchase lower-cost materials and components** from overseas, and thereby increase **gross profits,** and / or enable the business to **reduce prices** in order to **win sales / market share.**

In the context of importing supplies, there is scope for questions requiring an understanding of **exchange rates**. Remember, from Theme 1, KT the **exchange rate** is simply the price of one currency in relation to another currency. It affects the prices individuals and businesses pay for foreign goods and services.

Example:

A UK based company imports supplies from China. If the rate of exchange between British Pound (GBP) and Chinese Yuan Renminbi (CNY) is 1 GBP = 8 CNY, then the cost to the UK company, in British Pounds, for supplies from China priced at 10 000 CNY would be:

10 000 CNY / 8 = **£1,250.**

There is also scope for a question requiring students to explain how changes in exchange rates, expressed in terms of a **weaker or stronger pound**, may affect a UK business that **imports** supplies:

- A **weaker** pound (in relation to the UK business's overseas suppliers' currencies) will mean that the UK business will have to **pay more** for the supplies it imports from overseas. This will **increase variable costs** and, therefore, **raise break even level of output** and **reduce margin of safety and profit**, unless the business can **raise its prices without demand** for its products (or services) **falling**. In some cases, it may lead to KT **shrinkflation.** This is where a business reduces the size of a product but charges the same price, in order to cut costs and maintain profit margins.

- A **stronger** pound (in relation to the UK business's overseas suppliers' currencies) will lead to the reverse of the above; the UK business will **pay less** for the supplies it imports from overseas, which will **reduce variable costs** and, therefore, **reduce break even level of output** and **increase margin of safety and profit.** It may enable a business to charge **lower prices**, helping it to **win sales** and **market share.**

Exports (and the impact of exchange rates)

KT An **export** is a good (or service) leaving one country for another country.

Globalisation has enabled businesses to **sell to overseas markets** and, thereby, **increase sales** and more easily achieve objectives relating to growth and expansion. Higher levels of sales may also help to achieve **economies of scale** and with lower unit costs, a business can enjoy **higher profits** and / or be more **price competitive** and, thus, increase **sales.** As with imports above, there is scope for a calculation question on exchange rates.

Example: A UK based company exports its products to countries within the Eurozone. If the rate of exchange between the British Pound and the Euro is 1 GBP = 1.1 Euros, the cost in Euros, of one of its products priced at £15, would be 1.1 x 15 = 16.50 Euros.

There is also scope for questions on how changes in exchange rates, expressed in terms of **a weaker or stronger pound**, may affect a UK business that **exports**:

- A **weaker** pound (in relation to the UK business's overseas customers' currencies) will mean that these overseas customers will **pay less** to purchase the UK business's products and so they may be more able and willing to purchase the business's products. Therefore, the UK business may benefit from **increased sales** from customers overseas and, therefore, **higher overall profit**.

- A **stronger** pound (in relation to the UK business's overseas customers' currencies) will mean that these overseas customers will **pay more** to purchase the UK business's products and so they may be less able and willing to purchase the business's products. Therefore, the UK business may suffer from a **reduction in sales** from customers overseas and, therefore, **lower overall profit.**

Changing business locations

Globalisation has enabled businesses to change the location of their operations from one country to another country, and take advantage of **lower costs**, such as those associated with labour, raw materials and / or premises. These savings can enable a business to enjoy **higher profits** and / or to be **more competitive on price**, which can be crucial in **winning sales and market share.**

Multinationals

Globalisation has enabled businesses to set up or to buy additional operations in other countries. Companies that operate in several countries are called KT **multinationals**. Operating in countries where a business's customers are located will **avoid tariffs** (see below) being applied to the business's products. This is because the products will not be classed as imports, upon which tariffs may apply. This will help keep the **prices** of the business's products **competitive** in foreign markets, which will help **maximise sales.**

© Claire Baker - APT Initiatives Ltd, 2018

Barriers to international trade

Tariffs (and the effect on businesses)

KT A **tariff** is a fee levied on goods (or services) brought into a country. They increase the price of goods (or services) imported into a country. Therefore, they make it **more expensive** for a business to **import supplies** from abroad. This **increase in costs** will **reduce** the business's **profits**. It might also make it difficult for a business that exports **to compete on price** with **businesses located overseas** (due to higher costs), resulting in **lower sales**. Tariffs are, therefore, a **barrier to international trade** - as they make **foreign** suppliers **more expensive** than **domestic** suppliers, and this might result in a business using domestic suppliers over foreign suppliers.

Tariffs also make it **more expensive** for a business's **overseas customers** (where tariffs on imports apply) to purchase the business's products (or service). This will **restrict sales** to these markets. Tariffs are, therefore, a **barrier to international trade** - as they may result in a business's overseas customers choosing to buy **domestic products** over **foreign versions** of products, because the tariff **makes foreign goods (imports) more expensive**.

The main purpose of tariffs on imports is to **protect domestic businesses from competition from overseas**. However, this can result in domestic businesses being **less efficient** than they otherwise might have been, had the tariff not been applied. This is because tariffs make imports more expensive and reduce the need for domestic businesses to seek to **cut costs / increase efficiency**, in order to maintain competitiveness over price.

Trade blocs (and the effect on businesses)

KT **Trade blocs** are agreements between several state governments, where barriers to trade (such as tariffs) are reduced or eliminated among the participating states. Trade blocs can, however, be a **barrier to trade** as they often involve an agreement to apply **a common tariff** on goods **imported** into the **trade bloc** from **outside**. Such external tariffs **restrict opportunities** for a business located outside the trade bloc to sell to potential customers located within the trade bloc, as they may not be able to **compete on price** with businesses within the trade bloc. Major trade blocs include:

- European Union (EU)
- African Union (AU)
- Union of South American Nations (USAN)
- Caribbean Community (CARICOM)
- Central American Integration System (SICA)
- Arab League (AL)
- European Free Trade Association (EFTA)
- Eurasian Economic Community (EAEC)

How businesses compete internationally

The use of the Internet and e-commerce

The **Internet** and **e-commerce** provide opportunities for a business to sell its products / service(s) beyond its national boundaries and, therefore, to compete with businesses in other countries, **without the fixed costs** associated with setting up physical premises in countries overseas. Remember, from Theme 1: **KT** The **Internet** is a global network of computer networks, which connects individuals and organisations together and has enabled them to buy and sell their products or services online; **KT** **E-commerce** is the sale or purchase of goods or services conducted over computer networks. It has become most commonly associated with buying and selling products and services over the Internet ie 'online' through the use of electronic devices, such as desktop computers and laptops (and routers and modems) or, more recently, through mobile electronic devices such as mobile phones and tablets (and use of satellite technology).

Changing the marketing mix to compete internationally

Overview

Remember, from Theme 1, **KT** the **marketing mix** concerns the tactics a business uses in order to meet customer requirements and, ultimately, achieve marketing and overall business objectives. It consists of four basic elements: product, price, place and promotion. A business may need to change its marketing mix in order to compete internationally. This is due to **differences that exist between countries** across a range of factors, including differences in the following: language, currencies, climate, tastes and preferences, traditions and expectations, the timing of celebrations, disposable income, attitudes and beliefs, legislation and infrastructure. Numerous examples are provided below.

Changes to 'product'

A business may have to make changes to the **product** in order to compete internationally due to **differences in tastes and preferences**. For example, Asian countries have leaned towards 'salty and sour' as opposed to 'sweet' foods and Indian food is generally much spicier than English. Therefore, a business selling food abroad may have to adapt the ingredients used in products and / or develop new ones in order to accommodate different tastes, otherwise the product may not sell.

A business may also have to change the **materials / ingredients** used to make its products due to **differences in climate**. For example, some countries have climates that make them warm all year round and so products may need to be adapted to make them more heat resistant.

Changes to 'price'

A business may have to change the **price** of its products to customers in overseas markets due to **different currencies** - to take into account exchange rates, as these affect the price the foreign customer pays.

A business may have to change the **price** of its products to customer in overseas markets due to differences in **disposable income** (the amount of money people have to spend on goods and services). For example, in developing and emerging economies prices may have to be reduced (and / or product size and packaging reduced) in order to make products affordable within the target market.

Changes to 'promotion'

A business may have to change / translate the **wording used** in the **promotion** of its products - for example - in any advertising as well as on the packaging of products and on websites due to **differences in languages** - to enable the information and message conveyed to be understood by the foreign market.

A business may have to change its **promotional** material due to **differences in attitudes and beliefs** - to ensure the 'message' conveyed in its promotional campaigns does not conflict with the attitudes and beliefs held in the foreign country, otherwise the product will not sell.

A business may have to change its **brand / product name(s)** due to **differences in language** - if these are found difficult to pronounce, or translate poorly, that is, into words or phrases that have negative connotations in the foreign market, or do not convey what the product is about.

A business may have to change the **timing** of **promotional campaigns** due to **differences in climate / seasons**, or **the timing of celebrations**. For example, whilst it is winter in Europe, it is summer in Australia and so the timing of adverts promoting summer products would need to be different. In addition, Mother's day is not celebrated on the same day throughout the world, and so the timing of promotions relating to this would need to be different.

A business may have to use different **promotional mediums** to sell their products in countries overseas due to **differences in technological advancement / systems**. For example, some countries are less technologically advanced in terms of promotional mediums and use TV as opposed to digital and social media, and not all countries use the same search engines or social media.

A business may have to make changes to the **product and / or promotion**, including **packaging** due to **legislative differences** - for example - in terms of product labelling, safety, the environment and advertising.

A business may have to make changes to the **packaging** of its products due to **differences in traditions and expectations**. For example, in Asian countries such as China, India and Japan, gifting on special occasions including Valentine's Day is very popular, but in order to sell well, particularly amongst the Japanese, ornate packaging is expected, and this may necessitate investment in higher quality packaging.

Differences in currencies will also require changes to be made to any **promotional material**, including **websites with online ordering facilities** - to enable customers to know exactly how much the product / service will cost them in the currency with which they are familiar, as well as to pay for goods in their own country's currency.

Changes to 'place'

A business may have to use different methods of **distribution** due to **differences in infrastructure**. For example, not all countries have a well-established distribution network with centralised retailers, like Europe and North America. For instance, in China and India, the retail industry largely consists of many small, family-owned stores and street vendors. In addition, in India, methods used to reach consumers include rickshaws, bullock carts and boats.

Essential Knowledge Checklist

*Questions you should now be able to answer on **business and globalisation**:*

1. Define the following terms: a) globalisation b) imports c) exports d) exchange rate e) shrinkflation f) multinational g) tariffs h) trade blocs i) Internet j) e-commerce k) marketing mix.
2. Explain **one** impact of globalisation on a business.
3. Explain **one** way in which a business may benefit from each of the following: a) buying supplies from overseas (importing) b) selling to overseas markets (exporting)
4. Explain **one** way in which a weaker pound may affect each of the following: a) a UK business that imports supplies; b) a UK business that exports (sells overseas).
5. Explain **one** way in which a stronger pound may affect each of the following: a) a UK business that imports supplies; b) a UK business that exports (sells overseas).
6. Explain **one** barrier to international trade.
7. Explain **one** way in which a business may be affected by a tariff on the raw materials it imports.
8. Explain **one** way in which the use of the Internet and e-commerce can enable a business to compete internationally.
9. Explain **one** way in which a business might change its marketing mix in order to compete internationally.
10. Explain **one** reason why a business may need to change its marketing mix in order to compete internationally.

© Claire Baker - APT Initiatives Ltd, 2018

© Claire Baker - APT Initiatives Ltd, 2018

Ethics, the Environment and Business (2.1.4)

What you need to learn

The impact of ethical and environmental considerations on businesses:

➢ how ethical considerations influence business activity: possible trade-offs between ethics and profit; how ethical behaviour can be a source of added value

➢ how environmental considerations influence business activity: possible trade-offs between the environment, sustainability and profit

➢ the potential impact of pressure group activity on the marketing mix.

Introduction

KT **Ethics** are moral principles that govern a person's or organisation's behaviour. **KT** **Ethical business behaviour** is based on moral principles which guide decision making and govern the operation of a business. It concerns being fair and non-discriminatory in all business relationships, being honest and transparent, and showing consideration and respect towards the needs and interests of all those likely to be affected by the business's activities, as well as **the environment**.

The impact of ethical & environmental considerations on businesses

How ethical considerations influence business activity: possible trade-offs between ethics and profit

A business's ethical principles may influence a business to take action that **sacrifices profit**. Several examples are provided below:

* A business may decide to pay its workers **above the minimum wage**. This would **increase costs**, which would **reduce profit**.
* A business may decide **never to make use of child labour**. This would mean a business has to **pay more in labour costs** for adult workers, which **reduces profit**.
* A business may decide to **improve working conditions** for its employees over and above legal requirements. This is likely to **incur costs**, which **reduces profit**.
* A business may have a policy to **redeploy staff** instead of making staff redundant. This could incur **retraining costs** and any increase in costs **reduces profit**.
* A large business may decide **not to force a smaller supplier down on price**. This would mean that the **costs of its supplies are higher** than they might have been, which would mean **profit is lower** than it could have been.
* A business may decide to **donate** some of the **profit** it makes to local charities. This means **less profit** is available from within the business **for reinvestment** - for example - to fund future growth and expansion.

How environmental considerations influence business activity: possible trade-offs between the environment, sustainability and profit

There is growing concern over the environment and a business's ethical principles might extend to a business taking action that minimises the negative impact of its activities on the environment (such as pollution) and supports sustainability. **KT** **Sustainability** is the avoidance of the depletion of natural resources in order to maintain an ecological balance. Such action may, however, **sacrifice profit**. This is explained below.

Environmental considerations may result in a business **updating or investing in new equipment, machinery, systems** and / or **changing working practices** - in order to:

* **reduce the amount of waste** generated and, thus, reduce the amount of waste that has to be disposed of.
* **increase the amount of waste** that can be **recycled** and, thus, reduce the amount of waste that has to be disposed of.
* increase the proportion of **energy** generated from **environmentally-friendly sources**.

This will not only incur **one-off costs** associated with **buying** and / or **installing** or implementing the new technology / systems, but also the cost of **training** staff in how to use the new technology / systems. It might also result in **higher ongoing costs** and, therefore, **lower profits**.

Growing concern over the environment may result in a business reviewing the **source of its supplies** of materials / components used to make its products - to check they are from **sustainable** sources, and seeking alternative, sustainable sources of supply, where this is not the case. This might result in a business using **more expensive suppliers** and, thus, **higher costs**, resulting in **lower profits**.

Ways in which a business may benefit from acting ethically / more sustainably

In the **longer term**, acting ethically and / or implementing more sustainable working practices can be highly **beneficial** for a business. For example, it may create a **positive image** and generate **positive publicity** which, in turn, can provide the following benefits:

* It can help to **attract and retain customers** and, thus, help **maintain** or, even, **gain sales and market share**. This is because customers are increasingly taking into account business ethics and the extent to which businesses operate sustainable practices when choosing between alternative products / business services.

* It can make it easier to **attract and retain good staff**, thereby **minimising recruitment costs and labour turnover** and associated costs. This is because potential employees are increasingly taking into account business ethics and the extent to which businesses operate sustainable practices when applying for jobs.

- It can make it **easier to raise finance**, and thus secure the funds required for future plans / growth. This is because some investors will only invest in businesses with a good reputation in terms of business ethics / sustainable working practices.

Acting in an ethical manner and / or implementing more sustainable working practices may also provide **a source of added value**. This is because if a business operates more ethically or has more sustainable business practices than its competitors, and this is something which is valued by its customers, a business may be able to charge **higher prices**.

In addition, measures to control carbon emissions and reduce climate change, such as the use of sustainable sources of energy in the form of solar panels, wind turbines or hydropower, could also help a business **reduce costs** and **increase profits**. The price of solar panels has, for example, fallen significantly in recent years to the point where the cost of investing in them can be recouped in around six years and the savings after this point are likely to be substantial.

The potential impact of pressure group activity on the marketing mix

Remember, from Theme 1, **KT** **pressure groups** are organisations formed by a group of people with a common interest who come together in order to further that interest. This covers a wide variety of groups, including: trade unions, animal rights campaigners, environmentalists (eg Greenpeace), and trade associations who pressure the government to further the interests of their specific trade such as the Royal Institute of Chartered Surveyors (RICS) and the Confederation of British Industry (CBI).

Pressure groups can impact on a business that behaves in an **unethical manner** and may influence a business to **change elements of its marketing mix**. For example:

- In terms of **product**, pressure group activity may force a business to change the **materials** used to make its products in order to ensure they are more **environmentally-friendly**.

- In terms of **price**, pressure group activity may force a business to **raise** its prices as a result of **increased costs**. For instance, a pressure group may find out and publicise the fact that a business sources its supplies from a business that uses unethical and / or unsustainable working practices. This may force a business to use other, more expensive suppliers and, thus, to raise its prices to cover the **increased cost** (and, ultimately, maintain profit margins).

- In terms of **promotion**, any **negative publicity** arising from pressure group activity may force a business to invest in a carefully planned **public relations campaign** - in order to counter any claims of the pressure group, in an effort to persuade customers to continue to buy its products.

Essential Knowledge Checklist

*Questions you should now be able to answer on **ethics, the environment and business**:*

1. Define the following terms: a) ethics b) sustainability c) pressure groups.
2. Explain **one** way in which ethical considerations may influence business activity.
3. Explain **one** way in which growing concern over the environment may influence business activity.
4. Using a relevant business example, explain **one** possible trade-off between ethical business practices and profit.
5. Using a relevant business example, explain **one** possible trade-off between sustainable business practices and profit.
6. Explain **one** way in which operating ethically, or operating sustainable business practices (or being recognised as being environmentally responsible), may benefit a business.
7. Explain **one** way in which operating ethically or operating sustainable business practices can provide a source of added value for a business.
8. Explain **one** potential impact of pressure group activity on a business's marketing mix.
9. Discuss ways in which pressure group activity may impact on a business's marketing mix.

© Claire Baker - APT Initiatives Ltd, 2018

© Claire Baker - APT Initiatives Ltd, 2018

Topic 2.2

Making Marketing Decisions

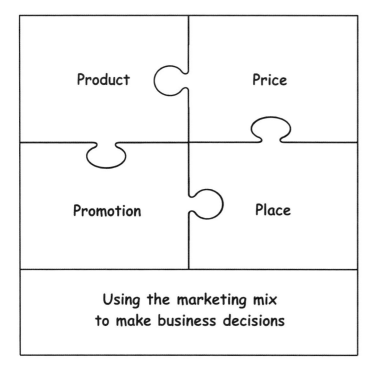

Product Price

Promotion Place

Using the marketing mix
to make business decisions

Product (2.2.1)

What you need to learn

The design mix:

➢ function, aesthetics, cost - how different elements of the design mix may be more important depending on the nature of the product being considered.

The product life cycle:

➢ the four phases of the product life cycle - introduction, growth, maturity and decline; recognition that the life cycle of a product is dependent on factors such as how dynamic the market is and how strong the product's brand name is.
➢ extension strategies eg lowering price, re-branding, re-positioning and increased advertising.

Product differentiation:

➢ methods of differentiating a product or service.
➢ reasons why it is important.

Introduction

When designing and developing new products, a business will seek to cut the **costs** of producing a product without reducing the **'value'** of the product from the **customer's** perspective, and / or to increase the **value** of a particular product (in the eyes of the customer) without increasing the **production costs**.

The design mix

Function, aesthetics, cost

Existing and new products can be assessed against three key criteria, namely:

- **Function** – This concerns what the product is supposed to be able to do - for example - the function of a kettle is to boil water.

- **Aesthetics** – This concerns how the product looks, for example, in terms of size, shape and colour – the extent to which it is 'pleasing to the eye'.

- **Cost / economy of manufacture** – This concerns the cost of producing the product, that is, the **direct** costs.

© Claire Baker - APT Initiatives Ltd, 2018
© Claire Baker - APT Initiatives Ltd, 2018

KT **Direct costs** are costs that directly relate to the production of a particular product or process. These include raw materials, packaging and wages of employees directly involved in producing / providing the product. Direct costs are also known as **prime** costs. They are usually the same as **variable costs**, but some **fixed costs** may be directly attributable to a particular product or process, for example, depreciation on production machinery.

Products are subsequently designed to:

- **maximise customer value.**
- **minimise the cost of production.**

The relative value placed by customers with regard to these areas will depend upon the **nature of the product** and **customers' individual needs and expectations**. For example:

- **Machines** in a factory need to be more capable of doing the job (**function**) rather than **aesthetically** pleasing.
- In **developed** economies - the emphasis for clothes may need to be more on **aesthetics** rather than **function**.
- **Cars** are often purchased according to their ability to satisfy **both** criteria equally, ie **function** <u>and</u> **aesthetics**.

Products are usually assessed by a mixed team of specialists in order to view them from all the required angles, including: designers, finance staff, and sales and marketing staff. This team of experts will:

- brainstorm all the essential **functions** that the product must be able to perform in order to satisfy customer requirements.
- consider the importance of **aesthetics** in selling the product.
- brainstorm as many ways of achieving these essential **function(s)** without affecting aspects relating to **aesthetics** considered important in selling the product.
- **cost** the alternatives.
- investigate the **cheapest** alternatives.
- select the best option.

The process usually requires:

- **market research** - to assess the opinions and perceptions of customers.
- the **production of prototypes** - to enable any products or product modifications made as a result of product (value) analysis, to be properly assessed.

The product life cycle

The phases of the product life cycle

Overview

KT The **product life cycle** refers to the different phases through which a product passes and the levels of sales experienced at each phase. Although these phases can be likened to the human life cycle, they are commonly known as:

1. '**Introduction**' (birth)
2. '**Growth**' (childhood and adolescence)
3. '**Maturity**' (adulthood)
4. '**Decline**' (old age).

The diagram below shows the four phases in relation to sales over time.

The Product Life Cycle

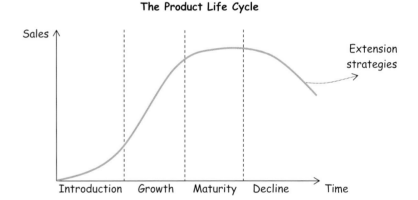

Note: Edexcel's Content guidance states that students will **not** be required to draw the product life cycle.

Factors influencing the life cycle of a product

No two products have identical life cycles. The life cycle depends upon:

- the **nature** of the product eg music albums and films have a short life.
- the **marketing policies** adopted and **how strong the product's brand name is**.
- how **dynamic the market is**, that is, how quickly **consumer tastes change**. This may, in turn, be dependent on the **pace of technological change**, which can quickly make once popular products **obsolete**. It also depends on **competitor activities**.

35

Introduction

This phase is where the product is launched into the marketplace. Price will be set high or low, depending on the **uniqueness** of the product and the business's **objectives**. If the product is **unique** then it may be **high**, otherwise it will be set **low** in an attempt to **build market share** before competitors enter.

There is usually significant investment in methods of **promotion**, particularly **informative advertising** - to raise awareness and educate customers about the product and its benefits. The more novel and complex the product the more promotion is required.

Throughout this phase, **sales** volumes are **low** (and, thus, capacity utilisation is likely to be low) resulting in **high fixed costs per unit**. Combined with high promotional expenditure, (particularly if this involves discounts to encourage sales), the business **may not make a profit** and **cash flow may be negative** (excluding support of external finance). Many products do not get past this stage.

Growth

During the growth phase, more and more customers become aware of the product and **sales** (and capacity utilisation) **rise**, resulting in **lower fixed costs per unit**. Promotional costs are also spread over a greater number of units. **Positive cash flows** and **rapidly rising profits** are, therefore, likely.

However, the **rise in profits** provides an **incentive** for **new firms** to enter the market. Competitors' costs may be **lower** as the key research and development has already been undertaken by the initial firm. Consequently, new firms may be able to **undercut prices** and, as a consequence, **take market share**. On the other hand, the 'originator' may have built up significant **brand loyalty** and have secured **key distributors** (eg retail outlets), making it difficult for competitors to persuade distributors to sell their product and secure a place in the market.

During this phase, changes are often required to **marketing strategy** in order to supply a **wider market** and **make it difficult for competitors** to secure a foothold:

- Price may rise or fall. It may remain **high or increase** in order **to recover development costs** and **maximise profits** before competitors enter. It may remain **low**, or **be lowered**, in order to **discourage competition**.
- If advertising has led to **high consumer awareness**, it may be **easier** to persuade any intermediaries used (eg retailers) to **stock** the product.
- Promotion is usually **persuasive** and includes the use of **special offers** in order to **build brand loyalty**.

Maturity

During this phase **sales** (and, thus, capacity utilisation) continue to **rise,** and thus **profits** continue to rise - as fixed costs are spread over more units. However, the **rate of growth slows** down and begins to level off, as **competition intensifies**. Promotion becomes **defensive** and there is **increased investment** in order to try to **maintain market share**, with emphasis on **branding and packaging**. It is during this stage that **extension strategies** (see below) are planned.

Decline

When a product is in decline, **sales fall** (resulting in low capacity utilisation), which leads to **falling profits**. The fall in sales is mainly as a result of **changing customer needs**, **new technologies** and / or **competitor activities**.

This stage may be **lucrative** if **marketing effort is withdrawn**, as this may significantly **reduce costs** and allow a firm to 'milk its product' for **profit** while sales slowly fall. However, if the product is thought to be **damaging to the company's image** or **reputation**, or **sales fall** to a level where **cash flows** become **negative** and the product is no longer making a **contribution to fixed costs and profit**, then it should be **withdrawn**.

Extension strategies

KT An **extension strategy** is a method used to extend the life of a product and is, therefore, usually implemented during the **maturity or early decline** stages of the product life cycle. Extension strategies include the following:

- **Encouraging existing customers** to **continue to buy the product over competitors** - through **lower prices, increased advertising** and / or **re-branding** and changing the design, image, appearance, packaging or ingredients slightly. *Toothpaste manufacturers* are constantly introducing 'new, improved' formulas. *Kellogg's* introduced a new range of *Cornflakes* called *Multi-Grain Cornflakes*.

- **Increasing the frequency of the product's use** - by **re-positioning** the product and, for example, emphasising the health benefits through **promotion**. For instance, *Mars* adverts have stated *"a Mars a day will help you work, rest and play"*. *Kellogg's* advertisements for *Special K Bliss* stated *"...a delicious new taste experience you can feel free to enjoy..."* with further information encouraging people to eat it at any time of the day... *"Indulge yourself in a heavenly combination of crunchy flakes and creamy textured cereal clusters, balanced with the lively tang of delicious raspberries and cranberries. And because it's from Kellogg's Special K, you can be sure it's low fat, so it's one indulgence you can really allow yourself, **whatever time of day.**"*

© Claire Baker - APT Initiatives Ltd, 2018
© Claire Baker - APT Initiatives Ltd, 2018

- **Attracting new users / targeting new markets for existing products** by **re-positioning** the product **through advertising.** For example, *Mars* began using athletes in adverts to attract athletes and 'sporty' segments. For the convenience market, *Kellogg's* introduced mini cereal bowls that contained one portion of cereal, UHT milk, and a spoon.

- **Developing alternative / new uses.** *Nylon* was originally used for military purposes in the manufacture of rope and parachutes. It was later developed as a fabric for women's stockings and clothes, and has since been incorporated into tyre manufacture. *Kellogg's* provides recipes for other food products on their cereal packets to encourage consumers to make new uses of their breakfast cereal - for example - *rice krispie* and *cornflake cakes*, which involves mixing together *rice krispies* (or *cornflakes*) with melted chocolate and golden syrup (or honey).

- **Introducing additional models / a wider range of products** - for example - *diesel engine versions for cars*. *Crunchie's 'white wine' flavour bar*, *Kellogg's* range of Special K products called *'Special K Bliss'*.

- **Extending the product into other formats** - for example - *washing powders* became *washing liquids*, *Mars bars* were extended into *ice creams*, *Kellogg's* introduced a *'Rice Krispies Square Chewy Marshmallow bar'* from their traditional *Rice Krispies.*

Product differentiation

Definition and methods

KT **Product differentiation** means making the product or service look different to those of competitors in the eyes of customers, and in ways valued by customers. There are two main **methods of product differentiation**, as follows:

- **providing actual product / service advantages,** that is, tangible / physical advantages. This may, for example, include making a product more effective or efficient in carrying out its function, or making it more visually appealing, or providing extra features or a more convenient location / easier access, faster delivery, longer guarantees / warranties, and / or more helpful, friendlier staff.

- **providing** *perceived* **product advantages,** that is, making customers believe that one product is better than another when there are no significant tangible / physical differences. This is achieved through **promotion**, in particular, **advertising, packaging, and branding.** For example, many advertisements attempt to create an image about a company or its product, with which the customer wishes to be associated.

The exact differentiation method used will depend upon the **target market**. With children's products, for example, businesses need to consider the customers (parents or carers) as well as the consumer (the children) in determining differentiation methods and, more specifically, the marketing mix to be used.

The harder it is for others to imitate the method(s) chosen for differentiation, the more successful a business is likely to be. In addition, the bases for differentiation must change in line with changing customer needs, as well as competitor activities.

Reasons why product differentiation is important for a business

Product differentiation is important in **maximising sales** and, therefore, **market share** and **overall profit.** This is because it helps to make a business's product **stand out from competitors,** and so more customers may buy the product over competitors' products.

Product differentiation is important in **maximising profits and profitability.** This is because it can help make a product appear **superior to competitors** in ways valued by customers, for which customers **may be willing to pay a higher price.**

Essential Knowledge Checklist

Questions you should now be able to answer on **product***:*

1. Define the following terms: a) product life cycle b) extension strategies c) product differentiation.
2. Give **one** element of the design mix.
3. Discuss the importance of aesthetics, cost and function within the design mix of a particular product or service.
4. Give **one** phase of the product life cycle.
5. Give the first / second / third / fourth phase of the product life cycle.
6. Give **one** factor influencing the life cycle of a product.
7. Give **one** extension strategy a business may use to extend the life of one of its products.
8. Explain **one** way in which a business may differentiate its product or service.
9. Explain **one** reason why product differentiation is important for a business.
10. Discuss the importance for a business of differentiating its product or service.

© Claire Baker - APT Initiatives Ltd, 2018

Price (2.2.2)

What you need to learn

Price

- pricing strategies - higher margin, lower volume versus lower margin, higher volume; reasons why businesses choose a given price - to reflect brand or product quality
- influences on pricing strategies: technology (eg gaming and freemium strategy, impact of price comparison websites), level of competition, market segments, product life cycle (methods relevant to each stage of the product life cycle).

Introduction

Remember, from Theme 1, **KT** **price** is the value of each unit of the product or service in the marketplace. It is the money the customer has to pay in order to buy the product or service, and it is the money the seller receives (the revenue) for selling the product or service.

KT **Pricing strategies** are courses of action relating to selling price required to achieve the business's objectives - for example - relating to level of sales, profit or market share.

Pricing strategies

High margin, low volume

Some businesses will charge a **higher price** in relation to other products or services in the marketplace (that satisfy the same need or want of consumers / customers), in order to position the product / service as a **'premium'** or **'luxury'** product / service (as opposed to 'economy' or 'no-frills'). They will only be successful in selling at the higher price if the product / service is considered to be **superior** to others in the marketplace, in ways that **customers value**.

Such a strategy will **restrict the number of people able and willing** to purchase the product / service and, thereby, **restrict sales volumes**. However, if the price is high in relation to costs, it will **maximise profit margins** (ie the difference between selling price per unit and cost per unit).

Some of the most widely known **luxury or premium brands** that use such a strategy are *Louis Vuitton, Gucci, Chanel, Rolex* and *Burberry*.

High volume, low margin

Other businesses, such as *Primark* and *Poundland*, will charge a **lower price** in relation to other products / services in the marketplace (that satisfy the same need or want of consumers / customers), in order to position the product / service as an **'economy'** or **'no-frills'** product, as opposed to 'premium' or 'luxury' brand. Such a strategy will **maximise the number of people able and willing to purchase** the product / service and, thereby, **maximise sales volumes** (and market share), but it will **reduce profit margins**. It involves minimising production and marketing costs in order to keep prices down and maximise sales volumes in order to generate sufficient profit.

Influences on pricing strategies

Cost (and size of a business)

'Cost' is not referred to in the Edexcel specification (or content guidance), but it should be appreciated that the **cost** involved in producing a business's product or providing its service is a key factor influencing the pricing strategy used by a business. In order to make a **profit** a business must sell its products / services at a **price** that **more than covers its total costs**. A business may be able to survive in the short-term by selling products at a price that at least covers the variable costs, but to survive in the long term total costs (ie fixed and variable) must be covered.

Still in the context of costs, it should be appreciated that the **size of a business** can influence the pricing strategy used. This is because large businesses have the ability to exploit **economies of scale** and, thus, benefit from **lower unit costs**. This enables them to **charge lower prices** than smaller businesses and still generate an **acceptable level of profit**.

Technology

Investment in **new technology** may enable a business to benefit from **lower production costs**. This will enable the business to sell its products at a **lower price** and, therefore, enjoy **higher sales** and **greater market share**.

New technology - in the form of **price comparison websites** - has forced businesses to **lower prices**, due to the ease with which consumers can compare products and prices between competing businesses.

Internet and digital technologies have also led to new pricing strategies, such as **KT** **'freemium'**. This is a pricing strategy where a basic product or service is provided free of charge, but money is charged for additional features relating to the product or service. This is common to digital products and applications such as software, media, games or web services.

© Claire Baker - APT Initiatives Ltd, 2018

Competition

The **level of competition** a business faces will influence its pricing strategy. This is because **price** provides a means of **directly comparing value for money** across all brands in the marketplace.

If **no close substitutes exist**, that is, no products that partly or wholly satisfy the same customer need or want as the business's product, then the business may be able to charge **a higher price**.

Where **close substitutes exist** (and it is relatively easy for customers to purchase an alternative product), then charging **a similar or lower price** than that of rival products may be essential to maintain and, hopefully, gain sales.

If competitors **reduce the price** of their products, then this may also prompt a business to **reduce its price**, in order to **avoid losing sales** to competitors.

Target market / Market segments

The business's **target market**, ie the **market segment(s)** the business aims its products / services at, will influence the pricing strategy used. Remember, from Theme 1, **KT** **market segments** are groups of customers within an entire market that share similar needs and wants and common characteristics. These may be based on how old they are, how much income they earn, where they live, hobbies and interests, etc.

A business cannot ignore the **price customers** within its target market **are willing to pay**, otherwise the product will not sell. This is largely dependent upon the **value customers place on the product / service**, and this value will depend on **the benefits** they feel it provides. A business may **increase the perceived worth (value)** of products / services (and, thus, the price it can charge) through **promotion**, in particular, through branding, advertising and packaging.

Product life cycle

Position in the product life cycle influences the pricing strategy used. **A high price** may be appropriate at **the start** ie the **introduction** phase - as consumers are attracted to owning a new product because it is perceived to appear or perform better in some way than existing products or services, and this may justify paying a premium price. During **maturity or decline** phases of the product life cycle, when **competition** is generally **greater** and becoming **more intense**, price may need to be **reduced** in order to **maintain sales** and **market share**.

Two alternative pricing strategies a business may use at the **introduction** stage of a product life cycle are outlined below.

KT **Price skimming.** This is where a new (or much improved version of a) product is sold at a **high price** for a **relatively short period** of time. The focus and main aim – at least in the short-term – is on **maximising** sales **revenue** and, ultimately, **profit** as opposed to sales **volume** and **market share**. Success is dependent upon customers being willing to pay a high price. Price skimming is common to **unique, innovative products**. The aim is to gain as much profit as possible while the product is unique and before competitors enter the marketplace with a similar product. It is used to target what are termed 'early adopters' of the product, that is, customers who are willing to pay a high price in order to get the product as soon as possible, because their need for the product, or understanding of the product's value, is greater than others, and so they are **less price sensitive**.

KT **Penetration pricing.** This is where a new product is sold at a **low price** in order to gain a **foothold** in the market. The focus, at least in the short term, is on sales **volume** and **market share**, as opposed to sales **revenue** and **profit**. The aim is to encourage people to **try** the product and to **secure brand loyalty**. The hope is either to **increase price** once brand loyalty has been established, or that **costs will fall**, and thus **profits will rise** to an acceptable level, as a result of **economies of scale**.

Essential Knowledge Checklist

*Questions you should now be able to answer on **price**:*

1. Define the following terms: a) price b) pricing strategies c) high margin, low volume pricing strategy d) low margin, high volume pricing strategy e) freemium pricing.
2. Explain **one** influence on pricing strategies / Explain **one** factor a business should consider when setting the prices for its products / service.
3. Explain **one** way in which each of the following might influence the pricing strategy used by a business: a) technology b) level of competition c) market segments d) product life cycle.
4. Explain **one** pricing strategy a business might use at the introduction stage of a product's life cycle.

© Claire Baker - APT Initiatives Ltd, 2018

Promotion (2.2.3)

What you need to learn

Promotion:

➢ appropriate promotion strategies for different market segments - benefits and drawbacks of: advertising, sponsorship, product trials, special offers, branding

➢ the use of technology in promotion: targeted advertising online, viral advertising via social media, e-newsletters.

Introduction

Remember, from Theme 1, within the context of marketing, **KT** **promotion** is communication techniques aimed at informing, influencing and persuading customers to buy or use a business's products or services. There are five main methods of promotion:

KT **Advertising.** This is the process of communicating promotional messages to customers through paid media eg through newspapers, television and radio.

KT **Personal selling.** This involves sales staff making presentations to, and / or taking part in discussions with, potential customers either face to face or via telephone or video / teleconferencing, with the purpose of making a sale.

KT **Sales promotion.** These are short-term incentives such as free samples / **product trials,** or **special offers** in the form of price discounts, to persuade customers to buy a particular product and / or distributors (eg retailers) to stock a particular product.

KT **Public relations.** This is about effectively managing relationships with different publics of significance to the business, mainly using news media such as press, TV and radio. Significant publics may include customers, employees and shareholders, as well as the government. PR activities include securing press / news releases, giving donations to charity, providing **sponsorship**, and obtaining product endorsements.

KT **Direct marketing.** This involves sending promotional messages direct to targeted customers ie without the use of other communication channels such as TV, newspapers, radio. It includes direct mail, email marketing, text messaging and telesales.

Branding is also often classed as a method of promotion. It should, however, be appreciated that it is much more than this. It concerns creating an identity for a business and / or its products which people recognise and which means something to them. This is not just created through communication techniques but through the product / service itself, the price of the product / service, as well as where and how it can be obtained.

Promotional methods are often classed as 'above the line' or 'below the line':

- **KT** **Above the line methods of promotion** involve techniques that communicate with customers (or other key stakeholders) through independent media, ie media over which the firm has little direct control and where there is no direct contact with the customer. This includes advertising on the television, in newspapers and on the radio, for example.

- **KT** **Below the line methods of promotion** concern techniques that do not involve independent media, but do involve the use of methods over which the firm has some degree of control such as direct mail and personal selling. These are commonly used for short-term tactical reasons, rather than long-term image building.

The method(s) of promotion used by a business will depend upon a number of factors - for example - the **cost** and **budget** available and, in particular, the **market segment** the business is aiming to target.

Appropriate promotion strategies for different market segments

Advertising

KT **Advertising** is the process of communicating with customers through paid media. A wide range of media is available to advertise a firm's products / services. These include business directories, newspapers, magazines, radio, television, cinema, posters and, more recently, the Internet. Within this range of advertising media available, there is scope to target specific **market segments**. For example:

- With **newspaper** advertising, there is scope to target specific **geographic** and **demographic segments.** For example, in terms of **demographic** segments, readers of the Sun newspaper differ in terms of **socio-economic** class to readers of the Daily Telegraph. **Geographic** segments can also be targeted through **local** newspapers.

- With **magazines** there is scope to target groups of people who have **the same hobbies or interests** (ie psychographic segments) **on a national basis.** This can be done by advertising in a magazine that is specifically read by the target market, or is likely to contain articles of interest to them.

- With **radio** advertising, there is scope to target **geographic, demographic** as well as **psychographic** segments: there are **local** as well as national stations, rather than regional and national (unlike commercial television); many stations target a specific **demographic** segment eg 35 to 54 year olds; different stations also cater for **different tastes in music** (psychographic segmentation).

- With **TV**, there is scope to target **geographic** segments - with the use of regional TV, as well as **demographic** and **psychographic** segments - by placing adverts during programmes known to be watched by certain groups. The increasing number of independent stations and specialisation of programs, now also provides scope to reach **niche market segments** who share particular beliefs, interests, opinions, etc.

- With **cinema** advertising, there is scope to target **demographic** and **geographic** segments. This is because different films are suitable for **different age groups** (eg U, PG, 12, 12A, 15, 18), and **local** adverts can be placed - for example - promoting complimentary activities such as **dining at a local restaurant**.

- There are 3 types of **poster** adverts: Roadside ie Billboard, Inside public transport (Buses, Underground), Outside Public Transport (Buses, Taxis) and with all three types of poster advert **geographic segments** can be targeted.

(Note: Advertising over the Internet / online is considered later below).

In terms of benefits and drawbacks:

In general, advertising is good for **building awareness** and can be effective at **reaching a wide audience** (unlike personal selling) and, thus, it is widely used for **fast moving consumer goods,** such as food items sold to the mass market. However, unlike personal selling and certain forms of direct marketing, advertising is **less targeted, impersonal,** and there is **more scope for the message to be ignored.** In addition, advertising does **not** provide the opportunity for **two-way communication.** Therefore, without the customer having to take further action (eg physically contacting the seller, unlike personal selling or telemarketing for example), there is **no** opportunity to **get immediate feedback, tailor the message, answer customer questions, get immediate action** and 'close' sales. In addition:

- There is a **one-off charge irrespective of the number of people who actually view the advert.** Thus, the business is paying for advertising which may not be seen or may not be effective in generating a response (unless it involves 'pay per click' advertising on the Internet).

- Adverts can be **seen by,** and thus **provoke a reaction from, competitors**.

- It is **difficult to measure the effectiveness** of adverts. Although sales rising directly after a campaign might indicate an advert was effective, on its own this does not tell you **how many** people out of all those people who read the newspaper, or listened to a radio station, or watched a TV channel that broadcast the advert, actually noticed the advert and understood the message it was trying to convey. Nor does it tell you how many of those people who actually noticed the advert and understood the message, **went on to purchase** the business's product **as a direct result of the advert** (unlike forms of Internet advertising, or other methods of promotion, such as personal selling and direct mail).

Sponsorship

KT **Sponsorship** is a form of public relations activity which involves funding for people or events, for example, relating to sports or the arts, in order to get a business's name or brand names associated with particular activities, and secure media coverage and awareness of the business and its product(s) or service(s). It enables a business to target market segments most likely to be interested in its products or services.

By sponsoring an individual, group or event **related** to the products / services that the business sells, the business is likely to benefit from **increased awareness** (amongst its **target market segments**) of the existence of its products / services, which can ultimately help **maximise sales / market share.** This is because sponsorship enables:

- **public exposure** of the business and / or its brand names and / or products **during** or **in connection with the event**.

- the business's name / brand names and / or logos and / or products to be **displayed prominently** at the event.

- **media coverage** of the event, which includes **sponsors' names and / or photos,** which might not otherwise have been available, or affordable.

Product trials

Product trials amongst a business's target market segment(s) can be a highly useful way to **assess consumer reaction** to its product / service in order to **identify any problems / weaknesses** and **allow improvements** to be made, if necessary, prior to a full launch, to ensure people buy it. It can also help a business to **forecast likely sales** of its product / service and, thus, **plan and organise the resources required to meet customer requirements** - for example - in terms of stock, staffing, cash flow, etc.

Special offers

KT Special offers are short-term incentives to encourage sales, such as discounts on first purchase, money off next purchase, buy-one get one free, 3 for 2. They can:

- encourage **potential** customers to **make their first purchase**.
- encourage **existing** customers to **buy again**.
- encourage sales at **'off peak'** times / out of season.
- make a product seem **better value** than competing products and this could help to **win sales from competitors**.

The main drawback of special offers is that they **reduce profit margins.** However, they can be crucial in **maximising sales** and **overall profit** of the business in the longer-term.

© Claire Baker - APT Initiatives Ltd, 2018
© Claire Baker - APT Initiatives Ltd, 2018

Branding

KT Branding involves giving a **distinctive** name, term, symbol, image, design or packaging to a product (or group of products), and this enables it to be **easily recognised** and **differentiates** it from other products.

Branding can be **highly beneficial** as follows:

- A strong brand can provide a business with a **competitive advantage** over rival businesses' products. This is because it helps to make a business's product(s) **stand out from others** in the marketplace. This is likely to lead to **more customers purchasing** the business's product(s) at the expense of rival brands, thereby helping to **maximise sales** and **market share**.

- A well-known brand can help a business **secure customers**. This is because people are more likely to buy a product under a brand name **they have heard of**. This is because a familiar name provides **reassurance** and **reduces the perceived risk** some customers experience when buying a new product.

- A strong brand may enable a business to **charge a higher price** for its products / service, thereby helping to **maximise revenues** and **profit margins / profitability**. This is because it can make a product **appear superior** in some way, and therefore customers may be willing to **pay a higher price**.

- Branding can help a business to **secure repeat business / customer loyalty** and, thus, **maximise sales** and **market share** over the longer term. This is because customers who like one product within a **particular brand** may be more willing to purchase another product with the same brand name.

- Branding can **reduce marketing costs**. This is because it enables the cost of marketing campaigns to be spread across a range of products, thereby exploiting **marketing economies of scale**. For example, an advert about *Cadbury* could help to increase sales of all chocolate confectionery products bearing the *Cadbury* name, at far less cost than advertising each product separately. Anything that minimises costs (without a corresponding fall in revenue) **increases profits**.

- Brand names have a **financial value** and, thus, can be included as intangible fixed assets on a company's balance sheet. Therefore, investment in branding can **increase the value of a business** and, thus, **the return on investment** for shareholders - in the form of a capital gain on shares if and when sold.

Branding can, however, be **costly**. This is because if often requires **considerable investment in promotion** - in particular advertising and packaging, in order to build an appropriate image that will attract and appeal to the target market.

The use of technology in promotion

Targeted advertising online

New technology enables website users to be monitored and tracked and, more specifically, information to be gathered on the user, including **what he or she searched for** and **where they are located** (from the IP address), in order to build up a **profile** of the user. This profile can then be used by Internet service providers (such as Google) to **target the user with adverts relevant to this profile** (which is essentially based on their search engine history).

Viral advertising via social media

KT **Viral advertising** is non-personal communication of information about a business or its product(s) / service(s) which spread like a virus, that is, very quickly from person to person, usually via **social media** networks - due to the ease and speed with which information can be shared.

KT **Social media** is web-based platforms, application and technology that enable people to socially interact with one another online. It concerns websites that contain content that users have created and posted themselves and / or that users can interact with / respond to. It includes *Facebook, Google+, Instagram, LinkedIn, MySpace, Pinterest, Snapchat, Twitter, WhatsApp, YouTube*.

Viral advertising via social media has the following key **benefits**:

- **Low cost**. With viral advertising, information about a business and / or its product(s) / service(s) can be posted on a social media platform, which is then shared by the user(s) of social media networks. This eliminates the need for the business to **pay for advertising**. Any reduction in costs **increases** a business's **profit**.

- **Wide reach**. With viral advertising, information about a business and / or its product(s) / service(s) can be posted on a social media platform, and this enables a business to reach a wider, even, international customer base, which can **significantly increase sales**.

Many businesses now have **apps** that existing and potential customers can download onto mobile devices. This allows businesses to **target customers** with offers that are **directly relevant** to them, and this can help to **maximise sales**.

© Claire Baker - APT Initiatives Ltd, 2018

© Claire Baker - APT Initiatives Ltd, 2018

e-newsletters

KT **e-newsletters** are publications that are distributed regularly to specific audiences (subscribers) via email.

Sending an e-newsletter is a much **less costly** method of promotion than a traditional newsletter. This is because, once typed an e-newsletter can instantly be sent to interested parties / the business's targeted audience via email and so, unlike a traditional newsletter, sending an e-newsletter **does not incur stationery** (eg paper), **printing** (ink cartridges) and / or **postage** (stamps) **costs**.

Essential Knowledge Checklist

*Questions you should now be able to answer on **promotion**:*

1. Define the following terms: a) promotion b) above the line methods of promotion c) below the line methods of promotion d) advertising e) public relations f) sponsorship g) sales promotion h) product trials i) special offers j) personal selling k) direct marketing l) branding m) targeted advertising online n) viral advertising o) social media p) newsletters.
2. Explain **one** way in which market segments can be targeted through advertising.
3. Give **one** benefit associated with advertising in general.
4. Give **one** drawback associated with advertising in general.
5. Explain **one** reason why a business may sponsor an individual, group or event related to the products / services it sells.
6. Explain **one** reason why a business might undertake product trials.
7. Give **one** reason why a business might use special offers.
8. Explain **one** benefit for a business of having strong branding.
9. Discuss the benefits for a business of having strong branding.
10. Explain **one** drawback for a business of branding.
11. Explain **one** way in which advertising online can be used to target customers likely to be interested in a business's product or service.
12. Explain **one** benefit for a business of using viral advertising via social media.
13. Explain **one** benefit for a business of sending e-newsletters over traditional newsletters.
14. Justify which method of promotion a business should use in a given situation.

Place (2.2.4)

What you need to learn

Place:

➢ methods of distribution: retailers and e-tailers (e-commerce, ie selling direct to the consumer via the Internet).

Introduction

The **'place'** element of the marketing mix is all about **methods of distribution**.

KT **Methods of distribution** refer to the different ways in which a business's product is made available to the end-customer or consumer (user). The end-customer could be members of the general public ie household consumers and / or other business organisations ie industrial consumers.

Some businesses **use distributors**, such as retailers (and / or wholesalers and agents). **KT** **Distributors** can be defined as business organisations involved in the process of making a product available to the end-customer or consumer (user). Other businesses **sell direct** to the end-customer or consumer, increasingly **via the Internet**. This may be through the website of an **e-tailer** such as Amazon, or through the business's **own (e-commerce) website**.

Methods of distribution

Retailers

KT **Retailers** are business organisations who buy direct from producers (or from wholesalers) for sale to the general public in shops or other retail outlets. Traditional retailers (as opposed to online retailers) are usually situated **near to where people live** to enable the public to easily access the products they provide.

Retailers often **advertise** the products they sell and **provide feedback** to the producers (and / or wholesalers) on customer **demand** and / or **reaction** to products. They **add on a profit margin** to the price they pay for the product from the producer (or wholesaler) before selling it on to the end-customer or consumer.

For members of the **general public / consumers**, besides providing **convenient access** to a wide range of goods, retailers provide **advice** and **after sales service**, and may also provide **credit facilities**.

There are a number of **benefits for a business** of using a retailer to distribute its products (as opposed to selling direct to the end-customer / consumer):

- Selling through retailers can be a **highly cost-effective way for manufacturers to reach a large and dispersed market.** It means that a business can sell its products nationally without having to invest in additional premises, staffing and stock – as the retailer provides storage facilities.

- Selling through retailers **eliminates the communication, administration, packaging and, in particular, transportation costs involved in receiving orders from and supplying individual customers / consumers directly.** This is because handling and processing the small order sizes involved in selling direct to individual members of the public / consumers could involve greater warehousing, stockholding and storage costs, as well as additional packaging, transportation, administration and communication costs, than the processing of bulk orders to retailers.

- Retailers **assist in the promotion of the product,** allowing the producer to **concentrate on production,** rather than marketing.

- Using traditional - as opposed to online retailers - also **overcomes some of the problems that can restrict online sales** - for example - the **lack of access** to, or **trust and confidence** in making purchases online, and the fact that some people may still prefer to **physically inspect products** before buying.

There are, however, **drawbacks** associated with using a retailer (as opposed to selling directly to consumers):

- The business has **less control over the price the end-customer / consumer pays** and may have to accept **lower profit margins** than selling directly to the end-customer / consumer. This is especially likely to be the case if the business sells through major, national retailers. This is because national retailers have considerable buying power which they can use to force down price.

- Selling through retailers may require **considerable promotional effort**. This is because competition for shelf space in retail outlets can be high, especially in major retail outlets such as the large supermarket chains.

- Retailers (as business customers) generally expect to **buy on** [KT] **credit,** that is, to have an interest free period in which to pay for goods (or services) received. Allowing customers to buy on credit **negatively affects cash flow**.

- A business selling its products through retailers is **not in close contact with the end-customer / consumer.** Therefore, it is likely to take **longer** for the business to become aware of, and **respond to changes in consumer needs, tastes and preferences**, which is crucial in maintaining a competitive advantage.

E-tailers (e-commerce)

[KT] An **e-tailer** is a business that sells goods or services via electronic transactions over the Internet. One of the most well-known e-tailers is *Amazon.com*, which opened its virtual doors in 1996, initially to sell books. It now sells a wide range of products and services and poses a significant threat to businesses in other retail sectors.

Since this time, many traditional 'bricks and mortar' retailers have decided to venture online, including department store - *John Lewis*, as well as the major supermarkets.

There are **benefits** for a business of using the Internet to sell its products / service:

- For a traditional bricks and mortar retail outlet, a website with e-commerce facilities may enable the business to **avoid investing in physical outlets** and, thus, benefit from **significantly lower fixed costs**, enabling it to **higher profits** and / or to be more **price competitive** and, thus, enjoy **greater sales** and **market share.**

- For a producer / supplier / manufacturer that has previously sold its products through traditional channels, such as a wholesaler or bricks and mortar retailer or agent, a website with an online ordering facility may enable the business to **bypass intermediaries / cut out the middleman** and **sell direct** to the end-customer / consumer, enabling the business to sell at a **lower price** than distributors, and thus to enjoy **greater sales** and market share and / or **higher profits** – as it cuts out the intermediary who adds on a profit margin before selling the goods on, which ultimately makes the price more expensive to the end-customer.

There are also **other benefits** associated with **direct sales** in general:

- The selling business is in **close contact with the end-customer / consumer** and, thus, is likely to be able to **respond more quickly** to changing customer requirements.

- There is an additional positive benefit of supplying direct to members of the **public** as opposed to other businesses, which concerns **cash flow**. Business customers, including retailers and wholesalers, generally expect to **receive credit**. When selling direct to the public, payment is likely to be made at the time the goods are received. A business may even be able to insist on payment in advance (depending on competitor terms) which is, obviously, better in terms of cash flow.

There are, however, **drawbacks** associated with selling direct to individual consumers:

- It may **require considerable marketing effort,** which can **take the focus away from production**.

- It can **significantly increase administration, stockholding and distribution costs.**

Indeed, compared to the cost involved in **processing bulk orders to intermediaries**, handling and processing the small order sizes involved in selling direct to individual members of the public / consumers, could involve:

- **greater warehousing, stockholding and storage costs.**
- **additional packaging, transportation, administration and communication costs.**

A business will only be able to offer a **more competitive price** and / or enjoy **higher profits**, if it is able to obtain **a certain level of efficiency in these areas**.

It should be appreciated that whilst some products can be **digitised**, others still need to be **physically delivered** to the customer. Obviously, for products that can be **digitised** eg *music, film, software* and even *airline tickets*, the above **costs would be minimal**.

Essential Knowledge Checklist

*Questions you should now be able to answer on **place**:*

1. Define the following terms: a) methods of distribution b) distributors c) retailers d) e-tailers.
2. Explain **one** benefit for a manufacturing business of using a retailer to distribute its products as opposed to selling directly to the end-customer / consumer.
3. Explain **one** drawback for a business of using a retailer to distribute its products, as opposed to selling directly to the end-customer / consumer.
4. Explain **one** benefit for a business of selling directly to consumers via the Internet.
5. Explain **one** potential drawback for a business of selling directly to consumers via the Internet.

© Claire Baker - APT Initiatives Ltd, 2018

Using the Marketing Mix to Make Business Decisions (2.2.5)

What you need to learn

How each element of the marketing mix can influence other elements.

Using the marketing mix to build competitive advantage - recognition that certain elements will be more important than others in determining competitive advantage, depending on the business context.

How an integrated marketing mix can influence competitive advantage.

Introduction

Remember, **KT** the marketing mix concerns the tactics a business uses in order to meet customer requirements and, ultimately, to achieve the business's objectives. It consists of 4 basic elements: product, price, place and promotion.

How each element of the marketing mix can influence other elements

How the 'product' can influence other elements of the marketing mix

The **nature of the product** can have a significant impact on other elements of the marketing mix. Numerous examples are provided below.

The materials and processes used to make the product are likely to influence the **price** charged. For example, if the product has to be made using expensive materials (and / or processes), then a high price will need to be charged in order to cover the cost of making the product and, ultimately, to achieve a certain level of profit.

How novel or unique the product is can influence the **price** charged. For example, the more unique the product, the higher the price that can be charged. This is because customers may be prepared to pay a premium price to be among the first or the few to own a particular product.

How simple / complex the product is to use or understand can influence the type of **promotion** used. For example, if the use and benefits of the product are fairly obvious / relatively simple to understand, then there would be little need to invest in intensive selling, promotion and product trials. However, for complex, technical products, personal selling and product trials may be essential to fully explain and / or demonstrate how a product works, as well as to reassure potential customers and answer specific questions.

© Claire Baker - APT Initiatives Ltd, 2018

The extent to which a product is affected by the seasons can influence the **promotion** used. For example, if the demand for and, thus, sales of a product is generally seasonal, such as ice cream or holidays in the UK, then a business may make use of **special offers** in order to boost sales at **off-peak** times.

The **nature of the product** can also have a direct influence on the **method / channels of distribution** used. For example:

- **Bulky** products need **direct** channels - as handling costs are likely to be higher.
- **Fragile** products need **direct** channels - to limit handling / the chance of breakages.
- **Perishable** products need **short** channels - to limit the chance of products going past their shelf-life before they reach the consumer.
- **Tailor-made** products need **direct** channels - as close contact with the consumer will help to ensure the product meets their specific requirements.
- **Technically complex** products need a **direct** channel - to allow explanations, questions and answers to specific questions.

Position in the product life cycle may also influence the **price** and **promotion** of the product. For example, a **high price** may be appropriate at **introduction** - as consumers who want to be at the forefront of owning a new product may be prepared to pay a premium price. During **maturity or decline**, when competition is fierce and sales are falling, price may need to be **reduced** - in order to maintain sales and market share. In terms of **promotion**, there is usually high investment at the **introductory** phase, particularly in **informative advertising** - to raise awareness of the product's existence and educate customers about product benefits, which is crucial in generating sales / building a customer base. During **growth**, promotion is usually **persuasive** and includes **special offers** - to encourage more people to buy the product and build brand loyalty. During **maturity**, promotion becomes **defensive** and there is increased investment to try to maintain market share, with emphasis on **branding and packaging**.

How the 'price' can influence other elements of the marketing mix

If a business sets a higher price for its products than other products in the marketplace that satisfy the same or similar consumer need (or want), then this will influence how and where the product is sold, ie the **'place'** element of the marketing mix. For example, **'premium'** priced products would **not** sell well in **budget / discount retailers** such as *Poundland*. They would be more appropriately 'placed' in **department stores** such as *Harrods* or *John Lewis*.

How 'promotion' can influence other elements of the marketing mix

Promotion may allow a **higher price** to be charged. This is because promotion (in particular, branding through advertising and packaging) can **add (perceived) value**, and can help to **differentiate a product** from rivals. It may help to convince consumers that they **need the product** and that it is **superior** to others in the marketplace, even though the basic product is the same.

How 'place' can influence other elements of the marketing mix

The **distribution** of the product can also influence the **price** of the product. For instance, if a business chooses to sells its products through **intermediaries** such as retailers instead of **direct** to consumers, these intermediaries will **need a return** on the products they sell. If the price these intermediaries are able to charge the end-customer / consumer is correspondingly low, and therefore generates a low gross margin, they may choose not to stock the business's products, (unless the business can lower its price).

If a business decided to **sell direct** to consumers via the **Internet**, it may be able to charge a **lower price** than a physical 'bricks and mortar' retailer, due to **lower fixed costs** (in terms of premises, staffing and stock).

Using the marketing mix to build competitive advantage

Overview

KT **Competitive advantage** is something that places a business above its rivals and may involve **lower prices, superior product offering** (eg longer lasting, more features / benefits), or **superior delivery of the product / higher levels of customer service** (eg faster delivery, more helpful, friendlier staff).

If a business is able to provide a customer with something over and above that of rivals, **that customers value**, then the business can be said to be **more competitive**, or to have **a competitive advantage**.

Lower prices

Lowering prices can improve a business's competitiveness - if the business can offer prices lower than competitors for a product that provides **similar benefits**. However, unless accompanied by **cost reduction**, lowering prices will **reduce profit margins**.

The ability to offer lower prices will depend upon the business's **costs**. The higher the business's costs in relation to competitors, the less able the business will be to offer lower prices. A business may seek to cut costs in many ways - for example - through **investment in new technologies,** and **training** and **incentives** to increase **productivity**.

Improving the product / service offering

Competitiveness can be improved by offering customers a product / service that provides **greater benefits** than rivals, such as better performance, extra features, better appearance, faster delivery, longer guarantees, etc. In the case of *mobile phones* - for instance - this could include the following:

© Claire Baker - APT Initiatives Ltd, 2018

- **better performance / functional superiority** – more hours of talk / usage time, bigger storage capacity / memory – speedier processor, brighter coloured display, less power consumption, more scratch resistant surface.
- **extra features** – including a camera, video-recording facility, projector, stereo FM radio, and Google apps.
- **better appearance / more aesthetically pleasing** and / or **fashionable** – providing a mobile phone in a wider variety of colours.
- **better after sales service and replacement package.**

Making the product / service offer appear superior through promotion

Competitiveness can be achieved by ensuring the promotion of a product is targeted precisely at the customer. Advertising can be particularly effective in making a product **appear superior** to others in the marketplace, even though there are no actual physical advantages. It can help to build images and brands with which the customer wishes to be associated. Offering incentives such as **free gifts** or **special offers** may also help to increase a business's competitiveness in the short term.

Making the product / service more easily accessible / widely available

Competitiveness can be improved by making the product available at **more convenient locations**, or at **more convenient times**.

The importance of market research

The most important point to emphasise about competitiveness is that it must be based on **what customers value** and that it (obviously) relates to **what rival firms are offering**. Thus, **research** into **what customers want** and **what competitors offer**, including analysis of their **strengths and weaknesses** in relation to the business, is vital in determining the most appropriate way(s) to improve a business's competitiveness.

How an integrated marketing mix can influence competitive advantage

A business will make decisions about each aspect of the mix, but the mix needs to be **blended effectively** to form **a unified whole** that **fulfils customer requirements** and, ultimately, **achieves the business's objectives** - in terms of sales, market share, profit, etc.

Some businesses may choose to focus on one particular aspect, for example:

- Some of the major supermarket chains, particularly *Asda* and *Tesco*, focused on **price** for a long time. *Tesco* has, however, re-positioned itself in the marketplace, placing emphasis on **product quality** through various promotional campaigns.

- With *detergents* and with *beers and lagers*, the focus is on **promotion**, with particular emphasis on television advertising.

All aspects will, however, still need to be addressed, as **all remain important** to the customer. Customers need a product / service that:

- meets their needs (product / service).
- they can afford / provides value for money (price).
- they are fully aware of and informed about (promotion).
- they can access conveniently (place / distribution).

If a business fails to address one particular aspect and / or **to ensure that each separate element supports and is consistent with** the other elements of the mix, then they are unlikely to be successful in the long term.

Essential Knowledge Checklist

*Questions you should now be able to answer on **using the marketing mix to make business decisions**:*

1. Define the term: competitive advantage.
2. Explain **one** way in which the nature of the product may influence each of the following elements of the marketing mix: a) the price of the product b) the promotion of the product d) the method of distribution of the product.
3. Explain **one** way in which the position of a product in the product life cycle can influence each of the following: a) the price of the product b) the promotion of the product.
4. Explain **one** way in which the price of a product can influence another element of the marketing mix.
5. Explain **one** way in which the way a product is promoted can influence the price of the product.
6. Explain **one** way in which the way a product is distributed can influence the price of the product.
7. Discuss how the nature of a product can influence decisions over other elements of the marketing mix.
8. Explain **one** way in which a business may build a competitive advantage using the marketing mix.

© Claire Baker - APT Initiatives Ltd, 2018

© Claire Baker - APT Initiatives Ltd, 2018

Topic 2.3

Making Operational Decisions

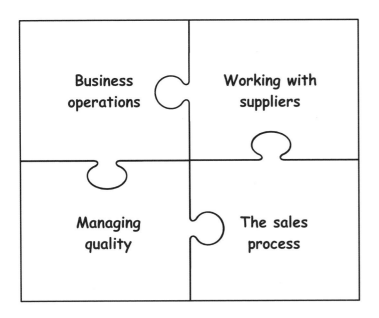

Business operations

Working with suppliers

Managing quality

The sales process

Business Operations (2.3.1)

What you need to learn

The purpose of business operations:

➢ to produce goods
➢ to provide services.

Production processes:

➢ different types: job, batch, flow
➢ the impact of different types of production process - the advantages and disadvantages: keeping productivity up, costs down, allowing for competitive prices.

Impacts of technology on production (ie the way businesses manufacture products):

➢ balancing cost, productivity, quality and flexibility.

Introduction

Remember, from Theme 1, the **role of business enterprise** and **the purpose of business activity** is to **produce goods** and / or **provide services**. These are made or provided using various **processes** and varying degrees of **technology**, and this has implications for **cost**, **productivity**, **quality** and **flexibility**.

The purpose of business operations

To produce goods

KT **Goods** (or **products**) are tangible (ie physical) objects that can be seen and touched such as cereal, shampoo, clothes, bicycles, computer games, mobile phones and pens.

To provide services

KT **Services** are things other people do for you such as cutting your hair, prescribing treatment when you are ill, getting you from one location to another (eg by taxi, bus, coach, train, ferry, plane), making you a meal, providing you with access to the Internet. Unlike goods, services:

- are **intangible** - they do not have a physical presence and so they cannot be touched, weighed or measured.
- require **a degree of interaction with the consumer** in order to be received.
- cannot be **stored**.
- are **heterogeneous** - the service a person receives is likely to vary to some extent, from one person to the next.

Production processes

Different Types

There are three different **methods of production** you need to learn about:

- **KT** **Job production.** This is where a single item is made (or order is processed), from start to finish, usually according to the customer's specifications. It usually involves 'one-off', unique orders which may or may not be repeated.

- **KT** **Batch production.** This is where a large or small quantity (batch) of the same item is produced at the same time. It does not involve the continuous production of items (as with flow production). It is appropriate when a limited number of the same item is required for a limited amount of time. Workers often **specialise** in one particular process, task or job. In the case of plastic toys, for example, this might include specialising in heating, moulding, assembling, sewing, decorating or dressing.

- **KT** **Flow production.** This is the continuous production of a large quantity of identical items. It often involves large investment in specialist machinery and is only appropriate when very large numbers and continuous supply of the same product is required (eg for mass market products where there is high demand).

The impact (advantages and disadvantages) of different types of production process

The impact (advantages and disadvantages) of job production

Advantages of job production:

- Job production provides scope to make things to **suit the exact requirements of the customer.** This may allow a business to charge **higher prices** (than with standardised products) - as customers may be willing to pay a premium for a 'one-off' product ideally suited to their needs. It also helps to **maximise customer satisfaction**, which is important in **maximising sales, market share** and **profits**.

- Workers may also be **more satisfied / motivated**, thereby **reducing labour turnover and associated costs.** This is because each job is **different** to the last and so workers may enjoy considerable **job variety** and have the opportunity to **utilise more of their skills.**

Disadvantages of job production:

- **Cost per unit is high**, due to the **high labour cost**. This is because workers are often **highly or multi-skilled** and the work tends to be more **labour** rather than **capital intensive**. There are also **limited opportunities for economies of scale.**

- **Flexibility** is also required - in terms of workers, machinery, and organisation - to ensure individual orders and short production runs can be dealt with.

The impact (advantages and disadvantages) of batch production

Advantages of batch production:

Unlike flow production (see below), batch production provides considerable **flexibility** in that it enables a business to **switch production** from one type of product to another type of product and, therefore, to make a **range of products** to **meet the needs** of a **variety of customers**, which could be crucial in **maximising sales and market share.** Batch production also results in:

- **higher productivity** (ie a greater number of products being produced in a given period of time) and **lower labour costs per unit** than job production. This is because workers often **specialise** in carrying out one particular task, and so they become **experts,** and thus **quicker** at carrying out this task.

- **improved quality / lower costs** associated with poor quality. This is because workers often **specialise** in carrying out one particular task, and so they become **experts** at carrying out these tasks, and thus make **fewer mistakes**.

- **lower unit material costs** than job production. This is because there is more scope for **economies of scale** - due to the larger quantity produced at any one time.

- **lower unit costs** (than job production). This enables a business to be more **price competitive** and / or to enjoy **higher profit margins.**

Note: **KT** **Production** is the process of transforming inputs into outputs. **KT** **Productivity** is a measure of how efficiently this process is being carried out. It can be defined as the ratio between outputs and inputs, such as the output of a given amount of capital or labour (eg number of items produced or number of customers served in a given period of time). It is measured by dividing the output by the input(s), such as the output of a given amount of capital or labour.

Example: If 80 production operatives produce 4,000 items a month, the (average) output per worker per month is: 4,000 / 80 = **50 units**.

The higher the output in relation to inputs **the higher the productivity** or productive efficiency. Factors affecting productivity include training, motivation, maintenance of machinery, planning and organisation (quality of management). In general, **the higher the productivity, the lower the cost**. A business can either **reduce prices** to customers to **gain a competitive edge** and **increase sales and market share** and / or enjoy **higher profits**.

Disadvantages of batch production:

- **Job satisfaction of workers may be lower** than job production. This is because the work carried out may not be **as varied**, as workers often **specialise** in one task.

- Like job production, batch production requires **flexibility** with regard to staff and equipment - to enable work to be **switched** from one batch of products to another.

© Claire Baker - APT Initiatives Ltd, 2018

© Claire Baker - APT Initiatives Ltd, 2018

- Compared to flow production, it is necessary to **clean down and / or re-set machinery** between batches. This is **unproductive downtime** when the machinery is not producing goods. Workers not involved in cleaning / re-setting will be **idle** during this period. In these ways, **productivity falls** and **average costs rise**.
- Producing a range of different batches of goods in any single day or week is, therefore, likely to require **careful production scheduling** - in order to achieve **high capacity utilisation** (ie maximise machine utilisation and minimise downtime between batches), as well as to match output with delivery times.

The impact (advantages and disadvantages) of flow production

Advantages of flow production:

Flow production benefits from **lower unit costs** than job and batch production because:

- processes are often **automated** and **machines** can be **less costly** to use than labour.
- workers employed in the production process require **little training / skill** - as they often **specialise** in one task, thereby **minimising training costs** and **wage costs**.
- large quantities are produced and so there is maximum opportunity to benefit from **economies of scale**. These will typically include purchasing economies of scale thanks to discounts from suppliers for buying larger quantities of materials.

With **reduced costs** a business can enjoy **higher profits** and / or offer **lower prices** than competitors, and therefore enjoy **higher sales and market share**.

Flow production can result in **improved quality**. This is because:

- processes are **automated** and **machines** are **more precise** and **reliable** than humans.
- production workers often **specialise** and, thus, **become experts** at their job and, therefore, **make fewer mistakes**.

Any improvements in quality may generate **positive word of mouth** and **favourable postings on social media**. This can help a business to **gain new customers** as well as **repeat business** from existing customers, thereby helping to **maximise sales, market share and overall profit**.

Flow production can also result in **increased productivity** (ie more products being produced in a given period of time). This is because:

- production is **faster** and set up in such a way as to ensure there are **no delays** between processes.
- processes are often **automated** and **machines** are **more precise and reliable** than humans, thereby **minimising delays** arising from **reworking** poor quality goods.
- workers employed in the production process often **specialise** and, thus, become **experts** at their job and are, therefore, **quicker** and make **fewer mistakes**.

Any increase in productivity may enable a business to **process orders** for customers in a **shorter space** of time, thereby **enhancing customer service** and helping to secure **repeat business**. Faster processing of orders may also help a business to **win customers** over **competitors**, as well as to **take on more orders**, both of which would help to **maximise sales** and **market share**.

Disadvantages of flow production:

- Flow production can be **expensive to set up** - due to the specialist equipment / machinery often required.
- It requires **very careful planning** - in the way the stages of production are organised and type of machinery needed - to make sure there are no hold-ups due to shortages of components.
- It requires **production line speeds** to be **carefully considered** and set at **optimum rates**, that is, speeds which encourage workers not to waste time but which allow them sufficient time to complete their work to the standard required.
- It can be **inflexible**. This is because a production line may be difficult to adapt once set up to produce a particular product.
- It can lead to **low job satisfaction** - due to the repetitive nature of the job - as workers tend to specialise in one particular task.
- If one part of the line breaks down **the whole line is affected** - production will have to stop until the line is repaired.

Impact of technology on production

Introduction - Types of technology used in production

Overview

KT **Technology** is the combination of skills, knowledge, tools, equipment, machines and computers used to undertake tasks. Types of technology used in production include **automation**, **robotics** and **design technology**. Each of these is briefly explained below, before considering the impact on cost, productivity, quality and flexibility.

Automation

KT Automation involves the **use of machines** (including **computers**) to carry out **operational tasks**. Automated machinery can range from simple sensing devices to robots (described below), and may concern one single task / operation, an entire process, or an entire factory. The latter is common to **KT** **mass production** - where large volumes of identical products are made to the same standard.

In the past, automation has largely been applied to carry out **manual, physical tasks** previously carried out by employees. The automation of **information** (as opposed to labour) is, however, now increasingly common.

Automation is most prevalent in **manufacturing**. For example, **KT** **computer-aided manufacture (CAM)** uses computers to control and adjust the production process. Automation can, however, also play a major role in **increasing productivity** and **reducing costs** in **service industries** - for example - the self-scanning checkouts in supermarkets. Automated stock control systems can also help to eliminate some of the **manual physical tasks** previously undertaken as well as assisting in **information processing tasks** relating to stock control. This is explained in the box below:

> **Modern stock control systems** consist of laser scanning devices that are used to scan the bar codes of stock items arriving into a business. This information is then passed to a central computer that stores details of the stock levels held. Any items leaving the business as sales or disposals (ie goods disposed of due to damage or going past their sell-by date in the case of food items), are also scanned, and the details fed back to the central computer - which automatically updates the stock figures held. Furthermore, with **EDI (Electronic Data Interchange)** the information on sales and stock levels held within a business can be passed to suppliers enabling orders to be generated automatically and deliveries to arrive as and when required ie 'just-in-time'.

Another example of how the processing of information is being automated includes **'Manufacturing Resource Planning' (MRP) software**, which enables management to quickly find out whether an order can be fulfilled with existing capacity, in the time available. This is because MRP software automatically calculates the labour, materials, machinery, and time required to complete a specific design / fulfil a specific order, and it compares this to the capacity and time available.

Robotics

KT **Robotics** involves the use of mechanical devices that can move automatically to carry out operational tasks unsupervised. **KT** A **robot** is 'a controlled reprogrammable multi-purpose manipulator' (ISO – International organisation of Standardisation) or, more simply, a mechanical device or piece of automated equipment that has three or more axes or degrees of movement. They operate by way of hydraulic, pneumatic or electrical power.

Robots were essentially created to reduce the need for humans to perform particularly **dangerous**, **dirty**, or **boring** and **repetitive tasks**. The main advantages of robots over humans is their **speed**, **strength** and **ability to withstand extreme conditions** that humans would find difficult to tolerate (eg extreme heat and the handling of hazardous substances), or that humans are able to tolerate but only with the use of expensive personal protective clothing.

Up until 20 years ago, robots were most commonly used in **car manufacturing**, but there are currently many different types of robot created for different uses. Industrial uses include **materials transport, welding, assembly, painting** and the **inspection and testing** of products.

Robots are also used in **environmental applications** – to clean contaminated sites, and in a range of non-industrial applications including **security** (airport surveillance), **commercial cleaning**, **food services**, **health care** (assisting the physically handicapped and the elderly, and supporting doctors and nurses in hospitals), and **space exploration**.

Design technology

Since the 1960's, modern information technologies have also been used in the **design** of products and services. **KT** **Computer-aided design (CAD)**, also known as **computer-aided drafting** involves the use of **computers** in the **design** process.

CAD software can be used to design two-dimensional (2D) and three-dimensional (3D) virtual models. It allows a business to simulate the product on a computer screen and to alter the specification, colour, features, in order to change the design, **without ever having to build a prototype**. It is extensively used in the design of **cars**, **ships** and **aeroplanes**, as well as **houses** and **commercial buildings**. For example, architects can use CAD to simulate the design of buildings and assess the engineering requirements. They can also simulate individual rooms and take the customer on a 'virtual tour', which allows customers to **modify their requirements** if required.

CAD is also used to produce **computer animation** for special effects in movies, advertising and technical manuals.

Impact on costs, productivity, quality and flexibility

Negative impacts

Implementing new technologies may incur significant **costs** - from **purchasing** and **installing** the new technology, as well as **training** employees how to use it.

Implementing new technologies may also mean that **some staff** are **no longer required** and so may necessitate **redundancies** (unless staff are able to be redeployed elsewhere). Redundancies can be **costly** (at least in the short term) in terms of **redundancy payments**. The longer staff have been continuously employed at a business, the higher the cost of making staff redundant. Redundancies can also result in **changes to work groups** and negatively affect the **morale and motivation** of staff who remain. This could result in a **drop in productivity** - at least in the short term.

There are also ongoing **running costs** but these costs should, in the long term, be **outweighed** by the benefits new technology can bring (explained below). The short-term issue is **securing the finance** required to implement the new technology. If this involves **borrowing** then there will be **increased costs** - arising from **interest payments**. In the long run, the new technology should more than pay for itself, otherwise there would be no point in implementing it.

© Claire Baker - APT Initiatives Ltd, 2018

© Claire Baker - APT Initiatives Ltd, 2018

Positive impacts

In the longer term, new technology is likely to **reduce costs**. This is because new technology may **reduce the need for staff** in general and / or for **highly skilled staff**, thereby **reducing labour costs**. With reduced costs a business can enjoy **higher profit** per item sold or **reduce its selling price,** which could help **gain sales** and **market share.**

New technology is also likely to **improve quality** <u>and</u> **reduce costs**. This is because new technology may enable products to be made with **fewer mistakes / greater accuracy,** thereby helping to reduce costs arising from **poor quality** (eg the cost of **re-working faulty goods, lost sales** arising from customer dissatisfaction / complaints) and / or the costs arising from the **removal of waste**. Improvements in quality may also help to generate **repeat business** and **new business** through **recommendations**, resulting in greater **sales, market share** and overall **profits**.

New technology may also enable a business to produce **more technically sophisticated products**, which may be important in **gaining a competitive advantage** and help **maximise demand** for the business's products, and thus its **sales** and **market share.**

New technology may enable tasks to be completed **more quickly** which, together with being **more precise** and **reducing or even negating the need for rework**, can increase **productivity**. Improvements in productivity may enable a business to develop new products or process orders for customers in **a shorter time** and, thus, reduce the **lead time** between an order being placed and customers receiving their orders. This could help a business to **win customers** over competitors, as well as enabling the business to **take on more orders**, both of which would help to **maximise sales** and **market share.**

Note: **KT** **Lead time** is the length of time taken between two or more processes - for example - between idea conception to product development and launch, between an order being received and delivered to the customer, or for a business to receive an order from a supplier.

One of the key points to make in terms of **productivity**, (which is particularly relevant to the use of **robots)**, is that, unlike humans, **machines do not get sick or ill** (with planned preventative maintenance), and **do not have feelings or emotions** that can negatively **affect their performance**, or the **satisfaction** gained from their work. Therefore, they are likely to be **more productive**.

In terms of other specific technologies, the benefits of **automated stock control systems** can be significant. Not only do they reduce the number of times stock has to be manually counted, thus **speeding up the ordering process** and **cutting labour costs,** they also help to:

- **minimise stock loss** – as greater accuracy of ordering leads to fewer reductions and disposals (caused by over-ordering).
- **minimise storage costs** – as up to date figures on stock levels enables faster ordering, and means less 'buffer' stock is required 'just-in-case'.

Furthermore, such systems can **help to ensure repeat business**. This is because more accurate ordering helps to minimise customer dissatisfaction arising from **poor availability** of goods, and the potential **loss in sales and profits** that result.

New technology through **CAM**, for example, also provides **greater flexibility**. This is because it enables different versions of the same product to be made within the same production run - for example - *motor cars* with different colours, models and engine sizes can be produced side by side.

CAD also **reduces the cost** and **time** involved in **new product development** (ie the lead time from idea conception to production). Therefore:

- CAD makes it **more affordable and feasible** for a business to invest in **new product development** and to investigate, test and modify a greater number of ideas than in the past, as well as to investigate **improvements to existing products**.
- CAD enables more **rapid response to changes in the marketplace,** ie to changing customer needs and feedback and competitor activities. This can be vital in helping a business to **gain a competitive edge** and, thus, **increase sales** and **market share.**

Essential Knowledge Checklist

*Questions you should now be able to answer on **business operations**:*

1. Define the following terms: a) goods b) services c) job production d) batch production e) flow production f) productivity g) lead time.
2. You should also be able to define the following: a) technology b) automation c) CAM (computer-aided manufacture) d) robotics e) robot f) CAD (computer-aided design)
3. Explain **one** advantage for a business of using each of the following methods of production: a) job b) batch c) flow.
4. Explain **one** disadvantage for a business of using each of the following methods of production: a) job b) batch c) flow.
5. Discuss the impact on (or the advantages and / or disadvantages for) a business of using each of the following methods of production: a) job b) batch c) flow.
6. Explain **one** impact improved technology may have on a business.
7. Explain **one** way in which improved technology may impact on each of the following for a business: a) costs b) productivity c) quality d) flexibility.

© **Claire Baker - APT Initiatives Ltd**, 2018

© **Claire Baker - APT Initiatives Ltd**, 2018

Working with Suppliers (2.3.2)

What you need to learn

Managing stock:

➤ the implications of holding stock (or more stock)
➤ interpretation of bar gate stock graphs - identification of: amount of buffer stock, maximum stock held, length of time it takes for stock to arrive once it has been re-ordered, the size of a given order
➤ the use of just in time (JIT) stock control.

The role of procurement:

➤ relationships with suppliers / factors that lead to the efficient procurement of raw materials: quality, delivery (cost, speed, reliability), availability, cost, trust
➤ the impact of logistics and supply decisions on: costs, reputation, customer satisfaction.

Introduction

Remember, from Theme 1 **KT** **suppliers** are individuals, businesses, or other organisations that provide resource inputs (eg raw materials, components, equipment, machinery, energy, fuel, etc) to other individuals, businesses or organisations that need them, in order to supply their customers with the goods or services they require.

Managing stock

Introduction to stock and the effective management of stock

KT **Stock (inventory)** is the raw materials and components, work in progress or finished goods a business holds at any one time. It can more simply be defined as any item stored by a business for use in production or sales.

Ideally, stocks should be kept **as low as possible** so that the **costs of holding stock** are **minimised**, but **not so low** that stock **runs out** and customer orders cannot be met.

The **costs of holding stock** include costs associated with **storage**, such as:

• the cost to **buy or rent premises** to store the stock.
• the cost to **heat and light** the premises where stock is stored.
• the cost of any **labour** required to **monitor stock** / protect it against **theft**.
• the cost to **insure** stock - against fire or theft.

A business may also have had to **borrow** to purchase stock, via an overdraft for example, (despite credit periods offered by suppliers). This is because it takes time to convert materials into finished goods, sell them and, ultimately, receive the money from customers. If so, the business will incur **additional costs** in the form of **interest payments**. Remember, any increase in costs **reduces profit**.

There is also an **opportunity cost** associated with holding stock, which concerns the fact that money tied up in stock cannot be released until that stock has been sold and paid for. **KT** **Opportunity cost** is what is sacrificed (or foregone) when one course of action is taken over another. In business, it is the value of the benefit(s) of the next best alternative course of action forgone, when making a choice between alternative courses of action. In the context of holding stock (or more stock) opportunity cost is, for example, the **interest** that could be earned on the money held in stock.

There are also other potential **risks and costs** associated with holding stock (or holding more stock) - It **increases the risk** of the following:

• **damage** – If employees know there is plenty of 'back-up' stock they may take less care when handling items, and so stock may become damaged and unable to be used in production (if raw materials), or sold on (in the case of 'finished' goods held).
• **theft / pilferage** - If employees know there is plenty of 'back-up' stock they might be tempted to take some for themselves, as it is less likely to be noticed as missing.
• **deterioration** - Stock may perish if held too long - in the case of fresh food eg milk.
• **obsolescence** - Stock of finished goods may become outdated / unfashionable if held too long, and thus unable to be sold on.

Despite the above costs and risks, a business may need to hold a certain amount of **(buffer) stock** at any one time for the following reasons:

• To **avoid running out of stock / reduce the risk of stockout** occurring. This would cause delays in production and result in customer orders not being met on time. This could result in loss of future business to competitors and / or late penalty charges - as a result of failure to meet customer deadlines, thereby reducing the profit made on orders.
• Because of **problems with the reliability of suppliers** in meeting delivery times and / or quality standards required by the business. These problems could result in the business not having enough stock to fulfil its own customer orders on time.
• To **ensure the business is able to meet a sudden increase in demand** and, thus, prevent the business missing out on extra sales. This could be crucial in achieving objectives relating to market share.
• Due to **difficulty predicting the level of demand** for its products. For instance, due to changeable weather conditions a business would not want to let customers down / miss out on sales should demand suddenly increase.
• To **secure bulk buying discounts** offered by suppliers. These help to keep down the cost of materials, resulting in higher gross profit on each product sold.

© Claire Baker - APT Initiatives Ltd, 2018

Interpretation of bar gate stock graphs

KT A **bar gate stock graph** is a diagram that shows the following:

- the maximum and minimum amount of stock to be held by a business at any one time.
- the point at which stock should be re-ordered.
- the re-order quantity.
- the time it takes for stock to arrive in the business after being re-ordered (the lead time).

An example of a bar gate stock graph for a business is provided below.

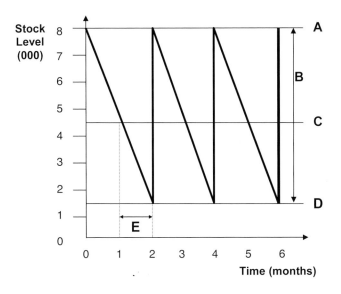

On the above bar gate stock graph:

- A is the **maximum stock level** held. This is **8,000 units** for this particular business.

- D is the **minimum (buffer) stock level** held. This is **1,500 units** for this particular business. The business may hold buffer stocks to avoid running out of stock - due to an unexpected increase in orders, or problems with delivery or work in progress, or to take advantage of discounts on bulk purchases offered by suppliers.

- B is the **re-order quantity**. This is **6,500 units** (8,000 - 1,500).

- C is the point at which stock should be re-ordered (the **re-order level**). This is when stock falls to **4,500 units**.

- E is the length of time it takes for stock to arrive once it has been re-ordered (the **lead time**). This is **1 month** for this particular business.

The use of just in time (JIT) stock control

Overview

KT **JIT stock control** involves materials and components arriving at the workplace just in time for use, and 'finished' products being immediately despatched to customers, with very little or no (buffer) stock kept in case of problems with delivery or work in progress, etc. To be implemented and work successfully JIT requires:

- **careful planning** including **accurate sales forecasting**.
- **flexible, reliable suppliers** – able to deliver more frequently in smaller quantities.
- **reliable machinery** – to ensure mistakes are not made and customer orders can be met. This has implications for maintenance and capital investment.
- **staff with the right ability, motivation and commitment** to ensure quality is right first time. This has implications for training, pay and other benefits.

Benefits for a business of using just in time (JIT) stock control

Only ordering stock 'just in time' for use can be **highly beneficial** for a business:

- It **reduces the costs of holding stock** (outlined previously above) - the costs of purchasing or renting storage capacity, insuring stock held against fire and theft, and financing stock held until money is realised from sales. This is because it keeps down the stocks of raw materials and finished goods held at any one time.

- It **reduces the risk of stock loss** - from stock being damaged, stolen, deteriorating / perishing, or becoming obsolete / out of date / unfashionable. This reduction of wastage keeps production costs to a minimum.

- It can **help to maximise quality and minimise waste and associated costs**. This is because it puts pressure on employees to check work thoroughly and get 'perfect quality first time', as there is no surplus stock to fall back on if mistakes are made.

- It can **highlight inefficiencies and enable timely improvements to be made**. This is because reducing the buffer stock makes any problems with delivery of materials, quality, machinery, training, etc more obvious, and this will prompt a business to make the effort to eliminate such problems.

- It **improves cash flow**. This is because it keeps down the stocks of raw materials and finished goods held at any one time, and so less money is tied up in stock.

- It **frees up storage space**. With minimum levels of stocks of raw materials and finished goods held at any one time, space might be used more productively to increase output, sales and profits.

- It might also **increase production workers' motivation**. This is because, with no spare stock to fall back on if mistakes are made, workers are likely to be given more responsibility to ensure products are right first time, and some workers might enjoy being given greater responsibility.

Drawbacks for a business of using just in time (JIT) stock control

There are a number of **drawbacks** associated with JIT stock control:

- It **increases the risk of delays in production / production halting** and, therefore, customer orders may not be met on time. This is because it leaves a business highly vulnerable to changes in supply and, thus, the risk of stockout occurring.
- It **restricts a firm's ability to meet a sudden increase in demand**, which might, therefore, restrict sales. This is because there is no spare stock and the business might not be able to receive additional stock in time to meet an unexpected surge in demand.
- It may mean the business **loses out on bulk buying discounts** offered by suppliers. This is because the business will be placing smaller, but more frequent orders with suppliers. This would increase the cost of materials, resulting in lower gross profit on each product sold.
- It **incurs greater administration / ordering and handling costs**. This is because the business will need to place smaller, but more frequent orders with suppliers and will have to deal with a greater number of smaller deliveries.

Before implementing JIT a business would, therefore, be wise to research whether the **lower stockholding costs** (storage, financing and opportunity cost), and **reduction in waste** stemming from the pressure to get **quality right first time**, were sufficient to **compensate** for any **loss in discounts** and would **outweigh** the **extra administration and labour costs** involved with handling a **greater number of smaller deliveries**.

The role of procurement

Introduction

KT **Procurement**, in the context of business studies, concerns finding and buying the goods and services a business requires in order for it to produce (or provide) its products (or services) to its customers. It is very much concerned with **building good relationships with suppliers**.

Remember, from Theme 1, a business is **dependent upon suppliers** to deliver the goods (and services) it requires to provide its product / service to customers in **the right quantity and quality**, in **the right place**, at **the right time**. Suppliers can, in fact, have a **major impact** on a business's **operational performance**, especially in terms of:

- the **quality** of the business's product / service and **level of wastage**.
- **unit costs**.
- **productivity** and **ability to meet customer orders on time**.

Relationships with suppliers - Factors which lead to the efficient procurement of raw materials

Quality

The **quality** of supplies is a key factor to take into account when choosing between suppliers. This is because the quality of a business's product / service is often largely dependent upon the **quality of the inputs** used to make / provide it. For instance, poor quality raw materials are likely to result in poor quality finished products and, thus, **increased costs** in terms of scrapping or re-working, and loss of customer satisfaction.

Delivery (cost, speed, reliability)

The **cost** to have supplies delivered, the **lead time** between an order for supplies being placed and goods being delivered, and **reliability** of a supplier - in terms of consistently delivering the right quality and quantity of supplies, at the right time in the right time place, are all factors a business may take into account when choosing suppliers.

The **shorter** the time it takes the supplier to deliver goods to the business once an order has been placed, the **less** will be the need for the purchasing business to order and purchase supplies in advance of using them and, thus, to **keep stocks of supplies**. Therefore, the **lower the stockholding costs**. There is also no point in choosing a firm because it is the **lowest cost** supplier, if it **cannot be relied upon** to deliver what is required, when it is required.

Location of suppliers

The **location** of suppliers has a direct impact on the **cost** and **lead time** for delivery. There are developing economies throughout the world where labour rates are not as high and sourcing supplies from such economies may help to ensure low cost supplies. A risk-averse business may, however, want to avoid using suppliers from overseas, despite lower prices (and, thus, costs), due to the **potential delays in delivery**, or risk of **exchange rate fluctuations** which affect the actual price paid. Furthermore, the further away the supplier, the more barriers there may be with regard to **communications**, and the more difficult it is to resolve issues relating to quality, specifications, etc, especially if it involves suppliers whose first language is not English.

Availability

A business obviously needs to avoid a situation where it has **insufficient supplies available** to produce its products / provide its service in time to fulfil customer orders. This might require suppliers to offer a **flexible service** in terms of order type, size, time, etc. This may be essential for a business **just starting out** when demand for its product / service is hard to predict accurately, as well as for **seasonable** businesses whose demand varies throughout the year.

© Claire Baker - APT Initiatives Ltd, 2018

© Claire Baker - APT Initiatives Ltd, 2018

Cost

Low cost supplies will enable a business to be **more competitive** over **price** and / or enjoy **high profit margins**. A business should try to exploit any opportunities for **discounts** on bulk purchases, or for **prompt payment** of invoices.

Trust

Trust is belief in the reliability, truth, or ability of someone or something. Within the supplier-business relationship, it is the belief that the supplier will deliver the right quality and quantity of goods in the right place at the right time. A great deal of trust will, obviously, be required if the business has **not previously used the supplier** and is asked to **pay in advance**.

Alternatively, if the purchasing business is given **KT** credit, ie an interest free period of time in which to pay for the goods after the goods have been received, it is the belief that the purchasing business will **pay** for the supplies **by the date agreed**.

It should be appreciated that supplies are often bought on **credit** and a supplier that offers **more generous credit terms** might win a contract to supply a business, even though its prices are **marginally higher,** because this facility **aids cash flow**. More generous credit terms may take the form of a longer credit period, or a lower interest rate charged on any accounts overdue.

Ethical and environmental considerations

Prompted by its employees, customers, lenders and investors, businesses are increasingly concerned about the **ethical and environmental consequences** of their decisions. A business may, therefore, refuse to use suppliers thought to be involved in any unethical activities such as the abuse of human rights - with unsafe working conditions, unfair wage rates, child or forced labour, for example.

The impact of logistics and supply decisions on: costs, reputation, customer satisfaction

Introduction - what is logistics?

KT **Logistics** is a process which aims to get the right item in the right quantity at the right time at the right place for the right price in the right condition to the right customer. It can more formally be defined as a process which involves planning, implementing and controlling procedures for the efficient and effective transportation and storage of goods (and services) from the point of origin to the point of consumption, in order to meet customer requirements.

© **Claire Baker - APT Initiatives Ltd**, 2018

Impact on costs

The lower the **price** suppliers charge the lower the business's costs, in particular, the lower the **unit costs**. For example, the lower the price of raw materials and components, energy and fuel, the lower the **variable costs** per unit. The lower the price charged by suppliers of leased equipment and machinery, the lower the **fixed costs** per unit.

Consistent quality supplies **reduce waste** through scrapping and re-working, and the associated costs.

Reliable suppliers can help to **maximise productivity** (and capacity utilisation), thereby minimising **fixed costs** per unit.

Flexible, reliable suppliers who are able to deliver supplies on a 'just-in-time' basis also play a significant part in reducing **stockholding costs**. However, as highlighted above, a reduction in overall costs will only be achieved if the reduction in stockholding costs is sufficient to outweigh the increased ordering and handling costs arising from receiving orders more frequently and the loss in any discounts on bulk purchases.

Generous credit terms from suppliers might also mean that a business can **rely less on the use of an overdraft**, which can be **costly** in terms of **interest payments**.

With lower unit costs a business can **reduce prices** to stimulate **greater demand** for its product / service and, thus, enjoy **greater sales and market share**, and / or it can enjoy **higher profit margins**.

Impact on reputation and customer satisfaction

As stated at the beginning of this topic, the **quality** of a business's product is very much dependent upon the **quality of the inputs** used to produce or provide it, in particular any supplies of raw materials used in the production of a physical, tangible product.

Furthermore, the **more reliable** the supplier is in delivering the quality and quantities a business requires, the more able the business is to meet its **delivery times** to customers.

Suppliers, therefore, play a big part in a business's ability to provide a product / service that **meets customer expectations** and, ultimately, in helping a business to gain an **excellent reputation** for **superior quality** and / or **faster delivery**. This is vital in **maximising sales** from **repeat business**, as well as in **gaining new customers** through **word of mouth recommendations**.

© **Claire Baker - APT Initiatives Ltd**, 2018

Essential Knowledge Checklist

*Questions you should now be able to answer on **working with suppliers**:*

1. Define the following terms: a) supplier b) stock c) bar gate stock graph d) just in time (JIT) stock control e) procurement f) logistics.
2. You should also be able to define opportunity cost.
3. Explain **one** disadvantage for a business of holding a large quantity of stocks of materials and / or finished goods.
4. Discuss the impact on a business (or implications for a business) of holding more stock.
5. Explain **one** reason why a firm might wish to hold buffer stocks.
6. Identify each of the following on a bar gate stock graph: a) amount of buffer stock b) the maximum stock level held c) the length of time it takes for stock to arrive once it has been re-ordered d) the size of a given order.
7. Explain **one** benefit for a business of using just in time (JIT) stock control.
8. Explain **one** drawback for a business of using just in time (JIT) stock control.
9. Discuss the impact on (or benefits or drawbacks for) a business of using just in time (JIT) stock control.
10. Explain **one** factor a business should consider when choosing between suppliers.
11. Explain **one** factor that leads to the efficient procurement of raw materials.
12. Explain **one** disadvantage for a business of making a poor logistical decision.

© Claire Baker - APT Initiatives Ltd, 2018

Managing Quality (2.3.3)

What you need to learn

The concept of quality and its importance in:

➢ the production of goods and the provision of services: quality control and quality assurance
➢ allowing a business to control costs and gain a competitive advantage.

The concept of quality

In law, a product must be 'fit for purpose' and 'as described' on any packaging or promotional material relating to the product. In everyday use, quality tends to mean a 'luxury' or 'top of the range' product. In business, quality is defined somewhat differently.

KT **Quality** is about providing the customer with a product or service that **meets their requirements and expectations** on a **consistent basis**. It does not necessarily relate to the most expensive or luxury good - as quality is 'in the eye of the beholder'. It is about doing the right thing in the eyes of the customer, and doing it right first time. It depends on customers' needs, expectations and perceptions. Customers determine quality and it is up to the management and the workforce to deliver.

The importance of quality in the production of goods and provision of services (in controlling costs and gaining a competitive advantage)

Minimising / controlling costs

Producing and providing quality goods or services is important to a business in **minimising costs** - for example - the cost of:

- **re-working re-testing, re-inspecting** poor quality goods - the cost of additional materials, labour and power used.
- **time spent handling complaints**.
- **legal action / compensation** arising from dissatisfied customers.

Maximising sales through repeat business and new customers

Producing and providing quality goods or services ensures **customers are satisfied** and, thus, can help **generate sales** through **repeat business** or **new customers** from positive word of mouth / comments on social media / customer recommendations.

© Claire Baker - APT Initiatives Ltd, 2018

Gaining a competitive advantage

Producing and providing quality goods or services can help a business **gain a competitive advantage**. If a business can improve its product over and above that of competitors, in ways that customers value, this can help to win customers from rivals. This may, even, enable **higher prices** to be charged - if the product or service quality is seen to be superior to a rival's, resulting in higher profit margins and overall profit.

Attracting and retaining good staff

Producing and providing quality goods or services can help a business to **attract and retain good staff**. This will make it easier and cheaper to secure the number of staff required to fulfil customer orders (and, ultimately, to meet business aims and objectives). It will also minimise labour turnover and associated costs. This is because staff are likely to prefer to work for a business with a reputation for good quality.

Concluding Remarks

Good quality is, therefore, important in **maximising efficiency** and **competitiveness** and, ultimately, in maximising a business's **effectiveness** in **achieving objectives** relating to **sales, market share, customer loyalty** and, ultimately, **profit**, which is crucial to a business's long-term survival. Producing **poor quality** products or providing a poor quality service can essentially lead to **the reverse** of the above.

Methods to ensure quality - quality control and quality assurance

What is quality control and quality assurance?

KT **Quality control** is the process of inspecting and testing products in order to reduce the number of rejects in the production process and returns from customers. It involves measuring performance against known standards, which should be based on customer expectations. These standards may relate to the behaviour of a person (if providing a service) or characteristics of a product (if manufacturing a product). With traditional quality control systems, the inspection and testing process has traditionally taken place **at the end** of the production process

KT **Quality assurance** involves more than the inspection and testing procedures associated with quality control. It involves a comprehensive, structured approach to quality, including planning for prevention. It involves devising systems to ensure defects do not occur in the production process. It includes external providers of goods and services and setting minimum quality standards for suppliers to meet, as well as identifying, discussing, selecting and implementing ways to improve quality on an ongoing basis. Unlike traditional quality control systems, it includes measures to check quality **throughout** the production process.

Differences between quality control and quality assurance

The basic difference between the two approaches is that **quality control** seeks to '**inspect out**' defects (defective goods), whereas **quality assurance** seeks to '**build in**' quality. The practical implication of this distinction is as follows:

- Quality **control** occurs **at the end** of the process (it is an 'end of the line' activity), whereas quality **assurance** occurs **throughout** the whole process.

- Quality **control** has, traditionally, been undertaken by **specialist quality control staff**, whereas quality **assurance** is **a matter for everyone** in the organisation.

- With the traditional approach to quality control (outlined above), **it is accepted that there will be some defects**, and that what is important is that they are detected before they reach the customer / consumer. The aim of quality **assurance** is to devise systems to ensure that **defects do not occur in the first place**.

- Quality **control** focuses on the **end-product** but quality **assurance covers all aspects** - from monitoring the quality of components bought in from outside, to procedures relating to the quality of customer service.

Concluding remarks

To conclude, **controlling quality throughout** the production process ie **quality assurance** can be **expensive**. However, it could ultimately **reduce costs** and, thus, make a business **more price competitive**, which could help **gain sales** and **market share**. This is because it is likely to result in **fewer**, if any, **defects** and, thus, **less wastage** relating to **reworking**.

Essential Knowledge Checklist

*Questions you should now be able to answer on **managing quality**:*

1. Define the following terms: a) quality b) quality control c) quality assurance.
2. Explain **one** reason why good quality is important for a business / Explain **one** impact on a business of producing high quality products.
3. Discuss the impact on a business of producing poor quality products.
4. Give **one** way in which quality control and quality assurance differs.
5. Explain **one** way in which quality assurance can help a business to control costs.
6. Explain **one** way in which quality assurance can help a business to gain a competitive advantage.

The Sales Process (2.3.4)

What you need to learn

The sales process:

➢ Product knowledge, speed and efficiency of service, customer engagement, responses to customer feedback, post-sales service; the impact on a business if an element of the sales process is poor.

The importance to businesses of providing good customer service:

➢ The impact this will have on the business, such as the impact on its brand, competitive advantage and the likelihood of repeat purchase.

Introduction - The sales process

KT The **sales process** is a systematic approach to selling which involves a series of steps, with the ultimate aim of making a sale. It **typically** involves the following steps:

1. **Prospecting** and **qualifying** - finding potential customers (prospecting) and determining whether they have a need for the business's product or service and whether they can afford to buy it (qualifying).
2. **Preparation** - preparing to make an initial contact with a potential customer. This is likely to involve preparing a presentation about the business and its product or service, tailored to meet individual customer needs.
3. **Approach** - approaching the customer either face to face or over the phone. This may involve presenting the customer with a gift, asking a question to gain interest, or giving the customer a free sample or trial to review and evaluate.
4. **Proposing / presenting** - actively demonstrating how the business's product or service will meet the needs of the customer.
5. **Handling objections** - listening to any concerns the customer may have and addressing them.
6. **Closing** - obtaining the decision from the customer to buy the business's product or service. This might require offering something extra - for example - the option to pay in instalments, a discount on the first order and / or stating that this offer is only available for a certain time period.
7. **Following up** - contacting a customer after purchase to obtain repeat business and referrals.

Note: The above steps differ to the elements of the sales process listed in the Edexcel specification. Those listed in the specification are, arguably, elements that help to make the above sales process effective (in generating initial and future sales).

Key elements of the sales process, including impact on a business if an element is poor

Product knowledge

Once a qualified lead (potential customer) has been identified, it is vital to **build customer interest** in the business's product / service. This requires **sound knowledge of the product / service**, in particular of the **benefits** it provides from the **customer's perspective**. If a sales person cannot clearly communicate the benefits of a product / service from the point of view of the customer, they are unlikely to **maintain the customer's interest** and, ultimately, **gain a sale**.

Speed and efficiency of service

If service is slow, or slower than a customer feels it should be - due to obviously incompetent staff and / or disorganised systems and procedures, a customer may **abandon their decision to purchase** a product or service. Ensuring speed and efficiency of service is, therefore, crucial in generating a sale.

Customer engagement

This is all about creating a **connection with the customer** that **drives them to purchase** the business's product or service and, ideally, to **continue purchasing** from the business after the sale has been made.

Responding to customer feedback and Post-sales service

To try to secure repeat business and new business from referrals, the sales process continues **after a sale** is made **(post-sales)**. This may involve the business asking customers whether they are **satisfied** with the product or service provided, and **responding to any feedback** received. This might require the business to address **any defects or issues** arising following the use of a product or service. If a business fails to do this, it is less likely to **gain repeat business** or **new business through referrals**.

The importance to businesses of providing good customer service

What is customer service?

KT **Customer service** is a series of activities designed to maximise the level of satisfaction that customers gain from purchasing a product or service from a business. It may concern the service given to customers before, during and after purchase, and it may be provided by a person, or through automated means.

Whys is good customer service important?

High levels of customer service can lead to **satisfied customers**. This, in turn, can result in a business gaining / benefiting from:

- **repeat purchases** / high levels of **customer retention** and **customer loyalty**. This is important in **maintaining sales** and **market share**.

- **new customers** - through word of mouth recommendations / positive social media posts from past and present customers. This is important in **building a customer base** and **increasing sales and market share**. It can help reduce investment in **paid promotion** to secure new customers and any reduction in costs can **increase profit**.

- **fewer complaints** and thus less time, effort and money wasted handling complaints.

- **a positive working atmosphere**, resulting in **increased staff retention** and reduced labour turnover and associated costs.

High levels of customer service can **improve a business's position and the way its brand is perceived in the marketplace** and provide a **competitive advantage**, which some customers may value more than price.

High levels of customer service can provide a **professional public image**. This may not only be important in **gaining customers**, but also in **attracting employees**, thereby **reducing time and money spent securing staff**. It can also be important in **attracting potential investors**, thereby making it **easier to secure the finance** required to implement improvements and / or plans for expansion.

Note, providing **poor customer service** is likely to result in the **reverse** of the above.

Essential Knowledge Checklist

*Questions you should now be able to answer on **the sales process**:*

1. Define the following term: the sales process.
2. Give **one** stage in the sales process.
3. Explain **one** impact on a business if an element of the sales process is poor.
4. Discuss the impact on a business if the sales process is poor.
5. Explain **one** reason why it is important for a business to provide good customer service / Explain **one** benefit for a business of providing good customer service.
6. Discuss the importance for a business of providing good customer service.
7. Discuss the impact on a business of providing poor customer service.

Topic 2.4

Making Financial Decisions

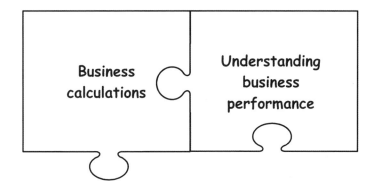

Business calculations

Understanding business performance

Business Calculations (2.4.1)

What you need to learn

The concept and calculation of:

➢ gross profit
➢ net profit.

Calculation and interpretation of:

➢ gross profit margin
➢ net profit margin
➢ average rate of return.

Introduction

Remember, from theme 1, **KT** **profit** is what is left from revenue after costs have been deducted from revenue: **Profit = Revenue – Costs.** If the figure is **positive** then a **profit** has been made. If the figure is **negative** then a **loss** has been made. There are several types of profit a business can calculate to assess its performance. For Theme 2, you need to be able to calculate **gross profit** and **net profit**, as well as **gross profit margin**, **net profit margin** and profit relating to an investment, namely, the **average rate of return (ARR)**.

The concept and calculation of gross and net profit

Gross profit

Calculation of gross profit (and cost of sales)

KT **Gross profit** is what is left from revenue after cost of sales have been deducted from revenue:

Gross profit = Revenue – Cost of sales

KT **Cost of sales** are costs that are directly involved in producing a product (or providing a service). These include the cost of raw materials used to make a business's product, and wages paid to production staff. Other terms for gross profit are **added value** and **total contribution**.

Example 1: If the revenue of a business is £378,540 and cost of sales is £165,380 then the gross profit would be: £378,540 - £165,380 = **£213,160**.

You could also be given figures for revenue and gross profit and be asked to calculate the **cost of sales**. An example is provided below.

Example 2: If sales revenue is £74.3m and gross profit is £39.6m, then cost of sales would be: £74.3m - £39.6m = **£34.7 million**.

Reasons for a fall in gross profit

A business's gross profit may **fall** as a result of:

• a **decrease in sales revenue**.
• an **increase in the cost of sales**.

A **decrease in sales revenue** could be caused, for example, by **increased competition** in the market(s) served by the business. This could result in the business being forced to **reduce prices** in order to maintain sales, which would reduce the difference between sales revenue and cost of sales (which is the figure for gross profit).

An **increase** in **cost of sales** could be caused by, for example, the business's **suppliers putting up prices**. This would increase the business's cost of sales, which would reduce the difference between sales revenue and cost of sales (the figure for gross profit).

Ways to increase gross profit

A business may increase gross profit by:

• **increasing sales revenue**.
• **reducing the cost of sales**.

A business might **increase sales revenue**, for example, by **increasing investment in promotion**. If cost of sales stay the same (or do not rise by the same amount as revenue) then gross profit will increase.

A business might **reduce the cost of sales**, for example, by **finding and using alternative, cheaper suppliers of raw materials** (though not at the expense of quality). Reducing material costs may be possible, for example, by making use of overseas suppliers in countries where labour costs are lower. If revenue stays the same (or does not fall by the same amount as cost of sales) then gross profit will increase.

Net profit

Calculation of net profit (and other operating expenses and interest)

KT **Net profit** is what is left from gross profit after other operating expenses and interest have been deducted from gross profit:

Net profit = Gross profit – (Other operating expenses + Interest)

Example 1: If gross profit is £213,160, other operating expenses are 124,180 and interest is £6,500, then net profit is: £213,160 - (£124,180 + £6,500) = **£82,480**.

87

You could also be given figures for gross profit and net profit and be asked to calculate the figure for **other operating expenses and interest**. An example is provided below.

> *Example 2:* If gross profit is £538,110 and net profit is £283,420, then other operating expenses and interest would be: £538,110 - £283,420 = **£254,690**.

Reasons to calculate net profit

There are a number of reasons why a business should calculate net profit:

- **To assess whether or not it is worth the business continuing**. This is because making a profit is the (main) reason why most businesses are established. It is the reward for the risks (financial and other), effort and time involved in setting up a business. Without profit, there is no reason for a business's continued existence, and therefore it would close.

- **To comply with legislation**. For example, limited companies have to calculate and submit details (and keep financial records) of net profit made to HMRC for Corporation Tax purposes. (This is a tax levied on company profits.)

- **To determine how much internal finance the business has available for investment**, to fund growth and expansion and / or investment in new technology for example. This source of finance does not incur a cost, as with loan capital.

- **To help secure external finance in the form of a bank loan.** By looking at a business's net profit performance banks can assess whether or not a business is likely to be able to meet the interest payments on the loan (and eventually pay the loan back). Banks generally require the net profit figure to be at least 3 to 4 times the interest payments.

- **To help secure investment from shareholders.** A consistent and rising net profit figure will help raise investment from selling shares, as this will reassure shareholders that they are more likely to receive a return on their investment - in the form of a dividend (ie percentage of profits after tax) on shares held.

Reasons for a fall in net profit

Like gross profit, net profit may **fall** as a result of **a fall in revenue** and / or an **increase in cost of sales**. If, however, there is no change in these figures and gross profit remained the same, then a fall in a business's net profit could be due to:

- a **rise** in any one of a business's **operating expenses**, for example, salaries of manager(s), rent on business premises.

- a **rise** in the **level of borrowing**, for example, an increase in the size of any loans or overdrafts - as this would increase the amount of interest paid (and net profit is calculated by deducting interest as well as a business's other operating expenses from gross profit).

- a **rise** in the **interest rate** applicable on any bank borrowing, as this would increase the amount of interest paid (and net profit is calculated by deducting interest as well as a business's other operating expenses from gross profit).

Ways to increase net profit

You could be asked to consider ways in which a business may seek to increase net profit, **other than** methods that seek to increase gross profit that is, methods to increase revenue or reduce the cost of sales. A business may, therefore, increase its net profit through:

- **measures that reduce other operating expenses**. For example, a business may decide to **move premises** to a location where the **rent is cheaper**; gross profit stays the same, but net profit will increase.

- **measures that reduce interest payments**. For example, a business may decide to **sell off any unused assets**, and **use the proceeds to reduce borrowing** and / or could shop around to get **cheaper interest rates** elsewhere; gross profit stays the same, but net profit will increase.

Calculation and interpretation of gross and net profit margins and average rate of return

Gross profit margin

KT The **gross profit margin** is the proportion of revenue left over after cost of sales has been deducted from revenue. It is calculated as follows:

$$\frac{\text{Gross profit}}{\text{Revenue}} \times 100$$

> *Example:* If revenue is £360,000 and gross profit is £216,000, then the gross profit margin is: (£216,000 / £360,000) x 100 = **60%**.

Changes in the gross profit margin could be due to **changes in revenue** and / or **cost of sales**. For example, a **fall in the gross profit margin** could be due to:

- an **increase in the cost of sales**. For example, a manufacturer might have incurred an **increase in the cost of raw materials** used to make its products. If sales revenue stayed the same then this would lead to a fall in the gross profit margin.

- a **reduction in sales revenue**. This may arise as a result of a **fall in sales volumes** or a **reduction in unit selling price(s)**. If cost of sales stayed the same then this would lead to a fall in the gross profit margin.

Net profit margin

KT The **net profit margin** is the proportion of revenue left over after all costs (ie cost of sales, other operating expenses and interest) have been deducted from revenue.

$$\frac{\text{Net profit}}{\text{Revenue}} \times 100$$

Example: If revenue is £360,000 and net profit is £79,200 then the net profit margin is: (£79,200 / £360,000) x 100 = **22%**.

A **fall in** the **net profit margin** could be due to:

- a **gross profit decrease** arising from a **fall in revenues** and / or a **rise in the cost of sales**.
- an **increase in other operating expenses**, for example, an **increase in rent on premises**. If gross profit stayed the same this would lead to a fall in the net profit margin.
- an **increase in interest paid**, for example, as a result of a **rise in the interest rate**. If gross profit stayed the same this would lead to a fall in net profit margin.

Average rate of return

KT The **average rate of return** (ARR) measures the return in terms of profit from a proposed capital investment. More precisely, it is the average profit earned each year over the life of a proposed capital investment, as a proportion of the total cost. It is calculated using the following formula:

$$\frac{\text{Average annual profit}}{\text{Cost of investment}} \times 100$$

Example: A business invests in new machinery at a cost of £500,000, which is expected to have a life of 5 years. This investment is anticipated to generate an additional total profit over the 5 years of £675,000. The ARR can be calculated as:

£675,000 / 5 years = average annual profit of £135,000.
Therefore: (£135,000 / £500,000) x 100 = **27%**.

ARR is a useful calculation to help **make decisions between capital investments**, such as extending a factory, purchasing new machinery, etc. Note: **KT** A **capital investment** is a long-term investment that requires a relatively large amount of finance in order to acquire, develop, improve and / or maintain a fixed asset such as land or buildings, a fleet of vehicles, or equipment.

Brief consideration of the impact of interest rates on a business's gross profit, net profit and ARR performance

Building on the impact of interest rates considered in Theme 1, it should be appreciated that a **rise in interest rates** could have a significant **negative effect** on a business's **gross profit, net profit**, as well as **ARR** performance. For example:

- A rise in interest rates could **negatively affect the demand** for a business's product and service. This is because people with mortgages have less money available to spend. This would result in **a fall in a business's sales revenue** which could, in turn, lead to a **fall in gross profit**. This is because, with lower sales, the business may **lose out on discounts** previously received from suppliers on bulk purchases of raw materials, thereby **increasing the raw material cost per unit**.
- A rise in interest rates could result in a **fall in net profit**, if the business has any **loans or overdrafts**. This is because it would **increase the amount of interest paid**. This extra cost, which is deducted from gross profit, along with other operating expenses, will result in a correspondingly **lower figure for net profit**.
- A rise in interest rates could also **reduce the return in terms of profit made on a capital investment (ARR)**, where the investment has been funded **using bank borrowing**. This is because it would **increase the cost** of the investment - in terms of **interest payments**, and thereby reduce the return on the investment.

Essential Knowledge Checklist

*Questions you should now be able to answer on **business calculations**:*

1. Define the following terms: a) gross profit b) cost of sales c) net profit d) gross profit margin e) net profit margin f) average rate of return g) capital investment.
2. Give the formula for calculating each of the following: a) gross profit b) net profit c) gross profit margin d) net profit margin e) average rate of return.
3. Calculate each of the following for a business in a given situation: a) gross profit b) net profit c) gross profit margin d) net profit margin e) average rate of return.
4. Explain **one** reason why each of the following may fall for a business: a) gross profit b) net profit c) gross profit margin d) net profit margin.
5. Explain **one** method a business might use to increase each of the following: a) gross profit b) net profit c) gross profit margin d) net profit margin.
6. Discuss methods a business might use to increase each of the following: a) gross profit b) gross profit margin c) net profit d) net profit margin.
7. Explain **one** reason why a business should calculate net profit.
8. Discuss the impact on a business of an increase in its cost of sales.
9. Discuss the impact on a business of an increase in operating expenses and interest.

© Claire Baker - APT Initiatives Ltd, 2018
© Claire Baker - APT Initiatives Ltd, 2018

Understanding Business Performance (2.4.2)

What you need to learn

The use and interpretation of quantitative business data to support, inform and justify business decisions:

➢ information from graphs and charts, which may include:
➢ financial data (eg sales revenue)
➢ marketing data (eg a percentage increase in sales volume)
➢ market data (eg average incomes).

The use and limitations of financial information in:

➢ understanding business performance
➢ making business decisions - figures used may be out of date or other limitations eg time period - demand is seasonal.

Introduction

This sub-topic focuses on the use and limitations of **quantitative** and **financial data** and **information** in understanding **business performance** and **making business decisions**.

KT **Data** can be defined as facts and figures from which information to aid understanding, assessment and / or decision making can be derived. **KT** **Information** is derived from data which has been processed, organised, structured or presented in a context so as to make it useful in aiding understanding, assessing performance and making decisions. Remember, from Theme 1, **KT** **quantitative business data** is data that can be **measured and expressed as a quantity**, that is, **numerically**. It may be expressed in a **graph, chart** or table and it may concern **financial, marketing** or **market data**.

Business performance can be assessed in terms of a business's ability to:

• fulfil its function and achieve its overall purpose, mission, aims and objectives.
• control costs, maximise sales and profits and meet short, medium and long-term targets relating to these.
• meet the needs of key stakeholders.

This sub-topic provides plenty of scope for students to be presented with quantitative data - in the form of a graph or chart or table - and be asked to make calculations and / or interpret the data to support, inform and / or justify business decisions.

The use and interpretation of quantitative business data to support, inform and justify business decisions

Use and interpretation of financial data

KT **Financial data** concerns facts and figures relating to the financial health of a business. This includes, for example, data relating to:

• the amount of **sales revenue** made by a business in a given financial period.
• the amount of **profit** made by a business in a given financial period.
• the amount of **cash** held by a business at a particular moment in time.
• the **value** of a business's **assets**, that is, the value of all the items a business owns.
• the **value** of a business's **liabilities**, such as the amount of money it has borrowed in the form of a loan from the bank.

Financial data is used by **management** to assess the business's **financial performance** and determine whether **action** needs to be taken to **alter / improve** the **business's performance**. Refer to the following bar chart for example which shows the amount of annual revenue generated by a business over a 3 year period:

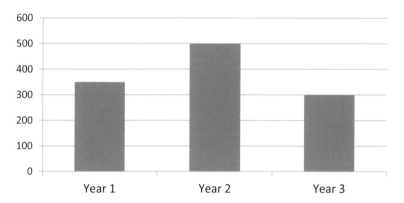

The bar chart shows that between Year 1 and Year 2 revenue increased by **£150,000** (from £350,000 to £500,000) and then fell to £300,000 in Year 3. This is a significant fall of **40%** between Year 2 and Year 3 [£500,000 - £300,000 = £200,000. (£200,000 / £500,000) x 100 = 40%] and the business should investigate why. The figures could also be used to calculate the average sales revenue for the business over the 3 years as follows: £350,000 + £500,000 + £200,000 = 1050,000 / 3 = **£350,000**.

Individuals and organisations outside a business such as **suppliers, potential lenders** and **investors** and **the government,** will also use financial data reported by the business to **judge its credit worthiness,** decide **whether to invest** in the business, and determine whether the business is **complying with government regulations** - for example - in terms of the **correct payment of taxes**.

© Claire Baker - APT Initiatives Ltd, 2018
© Claire Baker - APT Initiatives Ltd, 2018

Use and interpretation of marketing data

KT **Marketing data** can be defined as facts and figures that can be used to inform decisions over marketing strategy / the marketing mix, that is, decisions over product development, pricing, promotion and distribution. It may, for example, include:

- **Customer** data eg contact details, needs and preferences, interests.
- **Competitor** data eg revenues, products, prices, promotions, distribution channels.
- **Website** data eg number of visitors, pages viewed, bounce rate, sources of traffic.
- **Social media** data eg likes, shares, comments on any photos, videos or links shared.
- **Lead generation** data eg opt-in rates for newsletters or offers, email opens.
- **Sales** data eg number of transactions, sales volumes, total revenue per customer.

Such data would be crucial in **assessing the effectiveness of existing marketing strategy** and revising elements of the marketing mix (as required) to improve the business's performance in the future.

Use and interpretation of market data

KT **Market data** can be defined as facts and figures relating to the **size** of a market (in terms of volume or value), as well as factors that could affect the **demand** for and **supply** of a particular product or service (and, thus, the total size of the market for this particular product or service).

KT **Market size** is the total sales of all producers within a market, measured by value (sales revenue) or volume (units sold). Knowledge of market size is used by firms to assess whether a market is large enough to be **worth entering**, identify whether a market is **growing or declining**, and / or to calculate the **market share** of individual businesses within a market. Refer to the example provided below.

The total size of a market is worth **£8.6 million** in terms of revenue annually. Annual revenues for three of the leading businesses in this market are provided in the table below:

Business	Annual revenue
W	£2,580,000
X	£2,322,000
Y	£1,892,000

Using the information on **total market size**, each business can calculate its **market share** as follows:

- **Business W** (£2,580,000 / £8,600,000 x 100) = **30%**.
- **Business X** (£2,322,000 / £8,600,000 x 100) = **27%**.
- **Business Y** (£1,892,000 / £8,600,000 x 100) = **22%**.

Assuming there was only one other business supplying this market - **Business Z**, then the annual revenue and market share of this business could be calculated as follows:

Annual revenue: £8,600,000 - (£2,580,000 + £2,322,000 + £1,892,000) = **£1,806,000**
Market share: 100% - (30% + 27% + 22%) = **21%** OR £1,806,000 / £8,600,000 = **21%**.

One of the questions in Edexcel's sample assessment material required students to calculate the market share in terms of **actual value of revenue** for 3 businesses, using information on the total size of a market and percentage figures for market share. An example is provided below:

The total revenue generated by a particular market is **£170 million**. Only 3 businesses operate in this market and the pie chart below shows the market share percentage for each of these businesses.

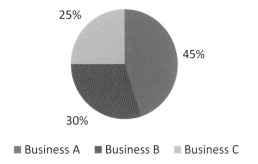

25%   45%

30%

■ Business A   ■ Business B   ■ Business C

Using the information provided, the market share of each business can be calculated as follows:

- **Business A** (£170m x 0.45) = **£76.5m**.
- **Business B** (£170m x 0.30) = **£51m**.
- **Business C** (£170m x 0.25) = **£42.5m**.

In terms of factors that could affect the size of a market, **average incomes** is provided as an example of market data in Edexcel's 'Getting Started Guide' (Content guidance). Data on average incomes might **influence business decisions** as follows:

- Data on average incomes might result in a business deciding to **expand or reduce** the **size** of its operations. For example, if average incomes are **rising**, then a business might decide to **expand** its operations. This is because rising average incomes means people have **more money to spend on goods and services** (as long as average incomes are rising faster than the rate of inflation).

The use and limitations of financial information

Use of financial information in understanding business performance and making business decisions

Financial information can be used to assess how well a business is performing in terms of - for example - the amount of **revenue** generated, or **profit** made in a given trading period, in relation to its objectives, as well as to **compare performance over time** (ie between different trading periods). This will enable the business to identify whether its performance is improving, worsening, or staying the same. This knowledge can then be used to **support, inform and justify decisions** over any **changes** required to business aims and objectives and / or how these might be achieved.

A business may use financial information to **compare its performance against other competitors** / businesses operating in the same industry or market, or against **industry norms**. Together with a comparison over time, this enables a more effective assessment to be made about a business's performance / potential performance. For example, a business's revenue and / or net profit may be increasing every year but when compared to other firms operating within the same industry, it may still be much lower, suggesting that there is room for improvement. This encourages further investigation to identify possible reasons for the lower performance and to help **make decisions** over **ways in which performance might be improved**.

Limitations of financial information in understanding business performance and making business decisions

Financial information does not inform the user about the **trading conditions** in which a business operates. This can lead to **inappropriate judgements** being made about a **business's performance**. For example, a well-established business may just about break even in one particular year and this might be considered poor performance. However, it might have taken a major improvement in productivity just to break even, if, for example, sales had fallen during a period of recession. Therefore, the business may actually be judged to have performed well, given the adverse external circumstances.

Inflation can lead to **inaccurate judgements** being made about a **business's performance**. This is because it distorts values over time. For example, growth in turnover may suggest growth in level of sales, yet the turnover might have grown due to prices rising and not due to an increase in sales volume.

Indeed, the main limitation in using financial information is that, on its own, such data **only shows** *what* has happened from a financial perspective, but **it does not tell you** *why* it has happened. Therefore, additional information, for example, on whether the business is seasonal, the trading conditions, inflation, the quality of human resources, etc is required to enable a full and accurate assessment of **a business's performance**.

Financial information can also **quickly become out of date**. For example, a business's working capital situation which reflects the values of stock, cash, debtors and creditors, can change on a day-to-day basis. Therefore, **conclusions about a business's performance** and **decisions over how it should respond**, based on a snapshot on one particular day in the year, may be **inaccurate / inappropriate**.

Other limitations of financial information in **understanding business performance** include the following:

- Businesses may **value their assets using different methods**, for example, how to value stock held or to allow for depreciation, and this can **make inter-firm comparisons** of business performance **difficult**.

- Businesses may have **different financial accounting periods**, which **makes comparisons** about one business's performance in relation to another business's performance **difficult**. For example, a toy manufacturing business reporting at the end of October, may have extremely high stock levels compared to a similar business reporting at the end of March, but this might be entirely normal given that the stock will reduce in the run-up to Christmas.

- Businesses might also **deliberately present a better picture** of their financial situation than is the case, by 'dressing up' their accounts. This is called '**window dressing**' and it leads to **overly optimistic** and, therefore, **misleading assessments** being made about **the business's performance**. Some of the ways in which businesses might do this reflect a broad interpretation of accounting rules; others are illegal, such as falsifying dates of costs and revenues.

Essential Knowledge Checklist

*Questions you should now be able to answer on **understanding business performance**:*

1. Define the following terms: a) quantitative business data b) financial data c) marketing data d) market data.
2. You should also be able to explain the difference between data and information.
3. Give **one** example of each of the following types of data: a) financial data b) marketing data c) market data.
4. Give **one** conclusion that can be drawn from a graph or chart in a given situation.
5. Explain **one** way in which a business might use financial information, such as information about its sales revenue or profit.
6. Explain **one** limitation of using financial information to understand business performance.
7. Discuss the limitations of financial information in understanding business performance or in making business decisions.

© Claire Baker - APT Initiatives Ltd, 2018

Topic 2.5

Making Human Resource Decisions

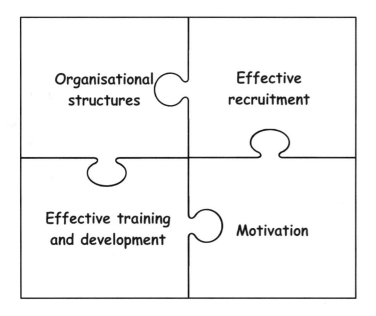

Organisational Structures (2.5.1)

What you need to learn

Different organisational structures and when each are appropriate:

➢ hierarchical and flat - difference between and when each are appropriate
➢ centralised and decentralised - difference between and when each are appropriate.

The importance of effective communication:

➢ why effective communication is important
➢ the impact of insufficient or excessive communication on efficiency and motivation
➢ barriers to effective communication, eg use of jargon / technical language.

Different ways of working:

➢ part-time, full-time and flexible hours
➢ permanent, temporary, and freelance contracts
➢ the impact of technology on ways of working: efficiency, remote working.

Introduction

KT **Organisational structure** refers to the way in which an organisation's activities are grouped together and coordinated to ensure members work together to achieve organisational goals. The way in which a business is organised can affect:

• the **motivation** and, thus, **performance** of staff.
• a business's **costs** and **profitability**.
• the **speed** with which a business is able to **respond** to problems and / or to changes in the business environment.

Organisational structure becomes increasingly important as an issue to consider as a business **grows in size** and **complexity**.

Different organisational structures and when each are appropriate

Hierarchical and flat

Definitions

KT **Hierarchy** is the order of levels of management or supervision within a business, from the lowest to the highest. **KT** A **flat organisational structure** has **few** (typically **up to three) levels** of management / supervision. **KT** A **hierarchical organisational structure** has **many** (typically **four or more) levels** of management / supervision.

© Claire Baker - APT Initiatives Ltd, 2018

© Claire Baker - APT Initiatives Ltd, 2018

In general, the **larger** the business in terms of **number of people** employed, the **more hierarchical** it will be. A local independent fruit and vegetable store is likely to consist of just two levels – the owner (and manager) and the sales assistants / staff. A large national company, on the other hand, may have many hierarchical levels, as follows:

Appropriateness, advantages and disadvantages

A **hierarchical** organisational structure may be appropriate for a business when a business **grows** - in terms of the **number of people** employed. This is because as more people are employed it becomes **more difficult to coordinate, control and optimise the use of business resources**. With additional managers / supervisors employed to fulfil this function, a business can **maximise productivity and efficiency**. There are also more opportunities for **promotion** than in an organisation with fewer hierarchical levels. This can help to **retain employees** and **motivate them** to work hard in order to secure a promotion. However, a **hierarchical** structure can result in the following:

- **problems with communication.** This is because the greater the number of levels, the longer it takes for messages to pass through, and the greater the opportunity for information to get distorted.
- **slow decision-making** and **slow response to problems / change.** This is because the greater the number of levels, the longer it takes for messages to pass through, and thus for problems to be identified and actioned upon.

In contrast, as long as the manager's **span of control** (ie the number of workers for which a manager is responsible) is not too wide, a **flat** structure can result in:

- **more effective communication.** This is because the fewer the number of levels, the less time it takes for messages to pass through, and there is less chance of information getting distorted.
- **faster decision-making** and **faster response to problems / change.** This is because the fewer the number of levels, the less time it takes for messages to pass through and, thus, for problems to be identified and acted upon.

Centralised and decentralised

Definitions

The terms **centralisation and decentralisation** refer to the extent to which the organisation as a whole, passes authority and responsibility for decision-making down into its divisions, departments and sections.

KT A **centralised organisational structure** is one where the **upper levels** of management in an organisation (typically based at a business's 'head office') hold the authority and responsibility for decision-making. **KT** A **decentralised organisational structure** is one where the authority and responsibility for decision-making has been **passed down** to people at lower levels.

Appropriateness, advantages and disadvantages

The **appropriateness** of centralisation (or decentralisation) depends upon the following:

- **The nature of the business and its activities.** If there is much similarity between a business's activities / operations, then centralisation might be more appropriate. This is because policies made centrally are likely to be relevant to each of the business's operations. And vice versa – if certain aspects of the business differ significantly to others, then decentralisation might be more appropriate.
- **Size and geographical spread of the organisation.** If a business makes a wide range of products for a wide range of markets across a wide geographical area, then decentralisation might be more appropriate. This is because few economies of scale are likely to be achieved from a centralised approach.
- **The environment in which the organisation operates.** If it is dynamic, decentralisation may be more appropriate - to be able to respond quickly to changes.
- **The risk involved.** The greater the risk involved, particularly with regard to financial decisions made within the organisation on a day to day basis, the greater the degree of centralisation likely.
- **The ability of employees.** Employees / lower level managers may not have the experience, skill or ability to cope with the extra authority and responsibility involved in decentralisation.

In terms of **advantages**, a **centralised** organisational structure can result in:

- **clear, unified vision / business aims and objectives.** A centralised organisational structure helps to ensure everyone works towards a common goal. (In contrast, a decentralised organisational structure could lead to a narrow departmental view).
- **greater control.** When a small group of people are responsible for all major decisions they retain more control over all aspects of the business.

- **greater uniformity / consistency** - in terms of policies and procedures. From a marketing perspective, this could be important in building a strong brand image which could, in turn, help to maximise sales.

- **less scope for conflict.** When a small group of individuals make the decisions, less potential exists for conflict to arise as a result of differences in opinion.

- **fast decision making.** With fewer people involved in decision making, decisions can be made much more quickly.

- **potentially better quality decision making.** Senior management have a holistic viewpoint and, it is argued, are likely to be more experienced and skilful. Hence, they are likely to make better quality decisions than those further down the organisation (although see additional advantages of decentralisation later below).

- **reduced costs.** This is because there is scope to benefit from economies of scale with, for example, bulk orders for items being placed by one central buyer, rather than smaller orders being placed by individual managers, which could result in the business losing out on discounts from suppliers. There is also less need to appoint specialist managers (eg separate HR specialists) throughout the organisation, since critical decisions are made by head office / the most senior staff, and then communicated throughout.

In terms of disadvantages, a **centralised** organisational structure can result in:

- **senior managers becoming overloaded with work issues.** This could result in them feeling stressed, which could negatively affect their morale and motivation, and ultimately lead to poor job performance. It could also result in poor communication with lower level managers, due to lack of time.

- **senior managers becoming more pre-occupied with their status than the needs of the business.** This could result in poor decisions being made, in the sense that they may not be in the best interests of the business and its shareholders.

- **slower response to problems / issues / change.** This is because requests have to be passed upwards and decisions awaited.

- **initiative being stifled.** This is because staff lower down the hierarchy may not bother to put forward ideas as they are not part of the decision making process. As a result, well-informed solutions to problems and ideas for improvement will not be considered and the performance of the business may suffer.

- **poor motivation amongst lower level staff.** A lack of responsibility for decision making can be de-motivating and stifles personal development. This may encourage the most able employees to seek better career opportunities elsewhere.

- **employees having less respect for their line managers** - if they see that their line manager cannot make decisions without referral to a higher authority.

The **advantages** of a **decentralised** structure are essentially **the reverse** of those cited as **disadvantages** of a **centralised** structure, and the **disadvantages** of a **decentralised** structure are essentially the reverse of those cited as **advantages** of a **centralised** structure. There are, however, **additional potential advantages** of a **decentralised** structure, as follows:

- **Better quality decisions** may be made. This is because more managers are involved who are likely to be better placed to make decisions over their sphere of operations, ensuring local conditions are taken into account. This can be important in maximising a business's performance.

- **Better quality managers** are also likely to develop. This is because managers throughout the organisation, not just at the highest level, have responsibility and authority for decision making. Therefore, they are likely to learn and develop from this experience and become better, more rounded managers as a result.

The importance of effective communication

Introduction

KT **Communication** is the process of transferring information between people. It essentially consists of six stages:

1. **Message conceived.** The sender becomes aware that there is a message to communicate and decides on the outline content.

2. **Message encoded.** The sender selects an appropriate 'language' (verbal or non-verbal) via which to communicate the message, and translates the message into words, symbols, diagrams, images or physical movement, ie body language.

3. **Medium selected and message transmitted.** The sender selects a medium eg informal chat, written report, memorandum and a 'tool' for transmitting the message eg telephone, email attachment, notice board.

4. **Message decoded.** The receiver 'reads' the message, which is hopefully in a 'language' that he / she recognises and is able to understand.

5. **Message interpreted.** Having understood the 'language' of the message the receiver deciphers the true meaning.

6. **Feedback provided.** The receiver sends confirmation to the sender that the message has been received and (hopefully) understood and correctly interpreted eg via a nod, smile, written acceptance or telephone call, etc.

Feedback is essential in letting the sender know whether the message has been received, understood and correctly interpreted. Failure to provide feedback could be **costly** to an organisation, resulting in, for example, incorrect deliveries which lead to delays in production and, ultimately, dissatisfied customers, lost sales and lower profit.

© Claire Baker - APT Initiatives Ltd, 2018

Reasons why effective communication is important

Ensuring customer and business needs are met

Communication is vital to business success as it is essential in ensuring that:

- employees are clear on their roles, tasks and responsibilities, and work towards achieving the business aims and objectives.
- decisions made by management are carried through.
- potential problems are identified at an early stage, allowing timely and appropriate action to be taken.

From a business's point of view it can help to ensure that, (along with training and appropriate supervision), tasks are completed to the **required standard** and by the **deadline set**, so **customer expectations** and, ultimately, **business objectives** are **met**.

Motivating employees

Providing employees with information about **what** needs to be done, **how** to do it, **by when**, is important in **relieving anxiety** and helping employees **feel safe / secure**. Giving them **feedback** on how they are performing is important in satisfying **esteem** needs / making them feel good about themselves (assuming the feedback is positive). Communication also requires the **interaction** of people and this can help to satisfy people's need to **socialise**. As a result of all the above, employees may feel **happier** at work and, thus, **more motivated** and, ultimately, they are likely to be **more productive**.

Devising and implementing strategy

Two way communication is important when planning and implementing strategy:

- At the planning stage, **customer research and feedback** is essential in determining the **most appropriate strategy(ies)** to implement.
- **Feedback** from **employees** on any proposals is vital in identifying **potential problems** at the implementation stage.
- Communicating the **reasons / potential benefits** for any changes in strategy at the implementation stage, can also do much to lessen **potential resistance**.

The impact of insufficient or excessive communication on efficiency and motivation

Introduction

KT **Efficiency** is all about minimising waste and keeping costs down. It is concerned with achieving objectives with a minimal use of resources, including time. A strategy is **effective** if objectives are achieved but if there was **extravagant use of resources** then it was **not efficient**. Only if the objective was achieved with no greater use of resources than the minimum necessary can we say that the operation was efficient.

KT **Motivation** is the driving force or process that compels people to choose a particular course of action. In a business context, motivation is not just about persuading a person to do a particular job but persuading them to **do it well**.

Impact of insufficient communication

If communication is insufficient, **employees will not be clear** on **what** needs to be done or **how** to do it, by **when**. This can result in **mistakes** being made and, thus, **inefficiency** - as time is wasted rectifying these mistakes. It could also result in employees feeling **anxious and insecure** which could negatively affect their **motivation**.

Impact of excessive communication

Excessive communication can lead to the following:

- **inefficiency / poor productivity**. This is because it can **take longer** to find key documentation when required, and **time and resources are wasted looking** for the information needed.
- **difficulty in prioritising**, and thus **failure to respond to urgent requests** / failure to **meet urgent deadlines**. This could have serious negative consequences for the business, for example, **financial penalties** or **lost sales**.
- **poor morale and motivation**. This is because it can lead to the receiver of the communication being unable to process all the information and, as a result, feeling **stressed** as they are unable to cope.
- **poor decision making or mistakes** being made. This is because it can result in the receiver **missing key information** as there is only a limited time to read, interpret and respond. This could result **in conflict**, **operational problems** and **inefficiency**.

Barriers to effective communication

Overview

KT **Barriers to effective communication** refer to factors that prevent a message from being received and understood or correctly interpreted.

Language barriers

Differences in **spoken language** between the sender and the receiver is an obvious barrier to effective communication. However, even when people speak in the same language, they can have difficulty understanding each other due to, for example, **regional accents**, or the use of **slang** or **jargon**. **KT** **Jargon** can be defined as vocabulary used by a particular profession or group that is unfamiliar to others outside this profession or group. These things can make it difficult for the receiver to understand messages correctly / cause confusion. This could result in mistakes being made, which could be costly for the business.

Physical / Environmental barriers

A **hot stuffy atmosphere** or room with **inadequate heating**, causing **discomfort** may lead to a **lack of concentration** and, thus, the message being **interpreted incorrectly**.

A **noisy** workplace may **hinder hearing** and **concentration** and, thus, result in a message being **interpreted incorrectly**.

Lack of privacy may cause **discomfort or embarrassment** and **distract the receiver** from **listening properly**.

Psychological barriers

Psychological barriers relate to the **psychological state of mind** of the sender or receiver. If, for example, the **sender** is **angry** or **stressed**, or suffering from **low morale** (ie a poor mental or emotional state), then this could result in he / she not taking the time to:

- compose a message carefully, resulting in vagueness and ambiguity.
- consider the receiver's abilities / limitations and thus, choose inappropriate language, resulting in the receiver not being able to understand.
- select an appropriate medium, eg tell someone bad news over the phone, when telling him or her face to face would have been more appropriate.

If the **receiver** is **angry** or **stressed** or suffering from **low morale**, then he / she may:
- choose to completely ignore the message received.
- be easily side-tracked or distracted, and thus fail to give the message his / her full attention.
- not take the time to understand the message eg by looking up words or concepts or asking for further explanation / clarification from the sender.
- not take the time to interpret it correctly, or deliberately misinterpret it.
- fail to provide the sender with feedback to reassure him / her that the message has been received, understood and correctly interpreted.

Physiological barriers

These concern the **physical state** of the communicators. For example, if the receiver suffers from hearing difficulties or poor eyesight, this could make it difficult for them to fully understand and correctly interpret a message.

Attitudinal barriers

KT An **attitude** can be defined as a mental view / opinion held by an individual or group of individuals which influences their behaviour. Attitudes concern our likes and dislikes and, as such, can help or hinder the process of communication. For example, if a **sender dislikes the receiver**, he / she may:

- deliberately **make it difficult** for a particular message to be **understood** - for example - by using **complex terminology** that the receiver does not understand.
- use **sarcasm** or **innuendo** or **over-simplified language** that the receiver is likely to find **condescending**.

Any of the above can **cause resentment** and could lead to the message being completely **ignored** and / or **incorrectly acted upon**. The receiver may also read what he / she expects and not what is actually there, resulting in **incorrect action** being taken. Likewise, if the **receiver** of a message **dislikes the sender**, then he / she may:

- put **less effort** into **decoding the message** to ensure it is **clearly understood**.
- deliberately **misinterpret the message** as a way of 'getting to' the sender.
- deliberately **limit their feedback** resulting in the sender not being certain that the message has been correctly understood or interpreted.

Furthermore, if the **subject** of the message concerns something the **receiver dislikes**, then they may be **unwilling to listen to the message** and **fail to act upon it**.

Structural / Systemic barriers

If **lines of communication** within an organisation are **not clear**, then this can make it difficult for messages to get passed to the correct individual.

Too many KT intermediaries, that is, people involved in helping to transmit a message from the sender to the receiver, could also lead to **excessive or long delays**, the original message becoming **distorted**, or the message **never being passed on**.

Constraints will also be placed on the communication process when the sender and receiver come from **different levels of the organisational hierarchy**. Communication with a **superior** may be rather **more formal and restrained** than it would be with an **equal**. For example, when an employee is consulted by the Managing Director the employee may only provide the answers that he / she thinks the MD would like to hear.

If receivers **feel alienated** and **lack commitment towards achieving business goals**, or their **personal goals conflict** with those of the sender and / or they share no common sense of purpose, they are **unlikely to be willing to listen** to new ideas. Alternatively, they may be willing to listen but **do not give the message their full attention** - as they **lack interest** in the subject matter or believe it bears **little relevance** to them.

Time constraints

Barriers relating to time, include the **time of day**, and **how long the sender and receiver have available** to deal with the communication. For example: If both parties are in **a hurry**, then **important points may be missed** and so communication may be ineffective; If it is late, at the end of a hard day's work, then **tiredness** may become a barrier to **decoding information** correctly.

© Claire Baker - APT Initiatives Ltd, 2018

Different ways of working

Part-time, full-time and flexible hours

Part-time hours

Working **KT** **part-time hours** involves working less than 35 to 40 hours a week. People are employed on a part-time basis for a variety of reasons, most obviously, **when there is insufficient work to employ someone full-time**. Part-time workers may, for example, be required to cover peak times, or unsocial hours (evening, Sundays only).

Employing people part-time increases a business's **flexibility** to meet **fluctuations in demand**. Job sharing in particular, can provide a business with flexibility as both parties may be able to be brought in at times of high demand. **Greater continuity** may also be possible with regard to **cover** in case of absence, holidays, etc. In addition, **different viewpoints** may result in **better quality decisions**.

Some people seek part-time work to fit in with **family commitments**. Employers are, in fact, **legally obliged** to seriously consider requests from parents with children under six to work part-time, and / or secure more flexible working including part-time hours. By offering part-time and / or more flexible working hours a business may, in fact, obtain the labour hours and skills it requires **much more easily** - by attracting skilled workers who are unable to work the standard full-time hours.

For the employee, part-time work can help to alleviate the **stress** involved in balancing **home life and work commitments** and can result in **greater job satisfaction, higher morale, lower absenteeism and lower labour turnover and associated costs**. This obviously has positive consequences for the employer - helping to **maximise productivity, performance** and, ultimately, **profitability**.

In the past, there was an additional reason for employing people on a part-time basis. This concerned the fact that part-timers acquired fewer employment rights than full-timers. This is now not the case, since **discrimination against part-time employees is an offence** under UK and EU law. Part-time workers have acquired more employment rights - for example - to training, holidays, and maternity / paternity leave (in proportion to hours worked).

Employing part-time employees over a full-time employee may involve **extra recruitment, training and administration costs**, but this may be offset by the potential benefits outlined above.

There are, however, other **potential drawbacks / difficulties** specifically associated with **job sharing**. For instance, it can lead to **conflict** and **poor motivation** because neither one person has complete ownership and accountability over the job. **Regular communication** is also essential to avoid **duplication of effort**.

Full-time hours

Working **KT** **full-time hours** involves working 35 to 40 hours per week. Obviously, it only makes sense to consider employing people full-time when **demand for a business's product or service provides scope to employ people on full-time hours**. If full-time hours are warranted, however, a business could always opt to split these hours between 2 or more part-timers, and so the question arises as to why a business might prefer to employ one full-time person over 2 or more part-timers to carry out a particular job. This is, largely, dependent upon the nature of the business and its customers, and the products or services it provides. For example, with **business to business transactions**, business customers may prefer to **build up a relationship with one individual** rather than several who **they can contact at any time** during a **standard working week**. The employment of a full-time person would, therefore, be appropriate in order to provide the service **customers expect / require**, and so **maximise customer satisfaction** and, ultimately, **sales**.

One of the **benefits** of employing people on a full-time basis is that they are likely to **carry out their job more quickly** than part-time workers and be **more able to handle any queries or unusual aspects** associated with the job. This is because they spend more hours of the working week at work and so are, naturally, **more experienced**.

Employing people on a full-time basis might, however, mean that during **off-peak** times they are **not fully utilised** and a business is paying for labour which it does not really need. Full-time employees also receive the **full range of employment rights**, although the gap between part-timers and full-timers has now been removed.

Flexible hours

Providing employees with the opportunity to work flexible hours can take several forms:

- **Flexitime.** This is where employees can **choose** (within certain limits eg between 7am and 11pm) **when to start and end each working day**, eg 7am until 4pm, 10am until 7pm, etc. It is commonly used for non-managerial office staff. Within this arrangement, staff may be allowed to work extra hours one day and take, say, half a day's leave the next. This is known as '**flexi-leave**'.

- **Compressed Working Weeks.** These allow an employee to **do a full-time job** in, say, **4 days instead of the usual 5**. The employee may, therefore, for example, work 7am until 6pm Monday to Thursday, enabling them to take **a long weekend**.

- **Term time contracts.** These are popular for parents, more commonly mothers, who do not wish to work in the school holidays, possibly due to difficulty in finding someone to look after their children and / or in funding the cost of childcare.

- **Self-Rostering.** Some businesses allow staff to **schedule their own weekly working hours**, as long as this fits in with the needs of the business.

© Claire Baker - APT Initiatives Ltd, 2018

Overall, as with opportunities to work part-time, flexible hours can help alleviate the **stress** involved in **balancing home life and work commitments** and can result in **greater job satisfaction, higher morale, lower absenteeism** and **lower labour turnover and the associated costs**. This, obviously, has positive consequences for the employer - helping to **maximise productivity** and, ultimately, **profitability**. Offering flexible working hours may also help a business to **recruit staff more easily** – attracting skilled staff who cannot work standard hours.

There are, however, some **potential drawbacks** for the business. For example:

- Offering **flexi-time** can **increase certain costs** such as **heating and lighting** and could also lead to **greater supervision costs**. This is because more than one supervisor may be needed to cover the longer working day.

- With **compressed working weeks**, care needs to be taken to ensure daily hours are not too excessive, as this could result in **fatigue** and **under performance**.

Permanent, temporary and freelance contracts

Permanent contracts

KT A **permanent contract** is one where an employee is contracted to work for an indefinite period of time. Employees should be hired on a permanent basis when the job they are required to do is likely to be required **indefinitely** in the foreseeable future, and they are **known** to **have the skills, qualifications and experience required** to fulfil the job requirements.

One of the **advantages** of employing staff on a permanent contract as opposed to a temporary contract is that they are, in general, likely to be **more motivated and committed** towards achieving organisational goals. However, permanent workers have **more rights** than temporary workers and so there is **less flexibility** and **additional costs** arising from their employment. For example:

- If a permanent member of staff has worked **continuously** at a business for a period of **two years** and they are **not performing** their job **to the standard required**, (despite being given adequate training and supervision), they **cannot instantly be dismissed**. A number of formal procedures have to be followed before dismissal can be regarded as 'fair' in the eyes of the law. This can **take time** and if the employer does not adhere to these procedures, this can result in **claims for compensation**.

- A member of staff who has worked **continuously** at a place of employment for **two years** is also entitled to **redundancy pay** should their job suddenly become obsolete and they cannot be re-deployed. The pay awarded depends on the length of time the employee has worked for the business. The longer the length of service, the higher the redundancy payment.

Temporary contracts

KT A **temporary contract** is one where an employee is contracted to work for a short period of time, usually under one year. Temporary workers are usually taken on to **cover seasonal peaks in demand, fulfil special projects,** or **cover short-term staff shortages** arising from holidays, sickness, maternity or paternity leave. They may also be taken on when there is **uncertainty** about **the future volume of business** and / or uncertainty about **the capability of the individual** being employed.

Temporary workers have **fewer rights** than permanent workers. Like all employees, they are legally entitled to:

- be paid the minimum wage.
- not be forced to work more than 48 hours per week.
- training to ensure their (and others) health and safety.
- not be discriminated against (ie treated unfairly eg on the grounds of race).
- take a certain number of paid holiday days per year.
- statutory sick pay - if they have worked for the same employer for over 3 months.
- maternity pay - if they have worked for the same employer for 26 weeks by the 15th week before the baby is due (and have earned a minimum amount per week).

However, they have **less rights** regarding **maternity / paternity leave, dismissal and redundancy**. The use of temporary workers, therefore, provides a business with:

- **flexibility** to cope with fluctuating demand.
- **cover** for staff at short notice.
- the extra labour hours / skills required **without** as many of the **legal obligations** associated with employing staff on a **permanent** basis.

The use of temporary staff can, however, prove **more expensive** than other methods to cope with fluctuating demand such as **overtime**. This is because it incurs **extra recruitment** (unless agency staff are used), **induction / training and administration costs**. Temporary staff might also, by their very nature, be **less motivated and committed** than permanent staff.

Freelance contracts

KT A **freelance contract** is one in which a self-employed individual or business is paid for undertaking a service and works under a **contract for services** rather than a contract of employment. The business is usually termed as a **client** rather than an employer. In contrast to employees, contractors usually **control the hours they work** and the **timing, tools** and **methods used** to complete a task, as well as **deal with their own income tax payments** and **NI contributions**.

The distinction between employees and freelance (or independent) contractors is of significance, and not just in relation to payment of income tax and national insurance.

Firstly, 'employees' acquire **legal rights** under the various Employment Acts. These rights relate to issues such as dismissal, redundancy, working hours, maternity and paternity leave, and payment of wages. An independent contractor is **not** an **'employee'** and, therefore, is **not covered** by the **full legal protection** (of the various Employment Acts) **given to employees**. Independent contractors will, however, usually be entitled to the **same rights** as employees with regard to **holiday** entitlements, along with their basic rights to **health and safety**, and **not** to be **discriminated against**.

The second main difference between employees and contractors is that it is a principle of English law that employers are **vicariously liable** for actions undertaken by employees in the normal course of their work. Therefore, if an employee causes injury through an accident to a member of the public, then not only is the **employee liable** in law, but so is the **employer**. Employers are **not vicariously liable** for the actions of **independent contractors**.

The main **reasons and benefits** associated with employing independent contractors are:

- Independent contractors provide a source of **readily available expertise** to undertake a **specialist task** that requires **skills that existing employees may lack** and / or that can often be brought in **at short notice** to cope with **seasonal** or **unexpected peaks in demand.**

- There are **fewer administrative duties and legal obligations** involved in employing independent contractors than those associated with employing people directly. For example, the business is not responsible for deducting tax or NI contributions.

- **Employers are not vicariously liable for the actions of independent contractors –** as explained above.

Drawbacks or difficulties arising from employing independent contractors:

- The use of specialist consultants and advisors **can be more expensive** than taking someone on as an employee with the necessary skills to fulfil a particular task on a temporary and, especially, permanent basis.

- If employees see expertise being brought in from outside and people being paid more for doing similar work, this may **negatively affect employee morale.**

- The business has **less control** over when, where and how independent contractors complete their work.

- Contractors may **lack the motivation and commitment** of permanent employees. For consultants and advisors that bill on an hourly basis, away from the workplace, there may be concern that they may not be working as productively as possible.

- There may also be **hidden costs** involved in employing independent contractors, for example, costs for parking and telephone usage. It is, therefore, obviously advisable to ensure all the costs associated with the use of a contractor's services are identified up front before any contracts for services are signed.

The impact of technology on ways of working: efficiency, remote working

Overview

KT **Remote working** is when employees carry out their job away from the employer's workplace. A growing number of people in certain types of jobs such as sales and marketing, accounting, proof-reading and editing, are working on a permanent basis **remotely**, many of them from home. This has been enabled through developments in information communication technologies (ICT), most recently high speed and wireless Internet connections.

Potential benefits of remote working

There are a number of potential **benefits** for a business of allowing its employees to work **remotely**. These are outlined below:

- Remote working (eg home working or teleworking) can **reduce a business's costs**. This is because it **avoids the need for office space** and, therefore, **reduces fixed costs** eg rent and rates. It can also reduce the cost of **travel expenses** (for the employer and employee) and reduces the need to invest in **social facilities**.

- Remote working can have a positive effect on **motivation**. This is because employees feel **trusted** to get on with the job which can **boost their self-esteem**. It can also help to **alleviate stress**, such as the stress associated with **commuting through rush hour traffic**. Any increase in motivation could **increase productivity**. (However, see potential disadvantages below).

- Remote working may also be **more productive**. This is because the employee may suffer **fewer interruptions / workplace distractions** and, therefore, be able to **complete more tasks** during their working hours.

From a **social / environmental perspective** the **reduction in travel** to and from work can also **cut down on air pollution**.

Potential drawbacks of remote working

On the **negative** side:

- It can be **expensive** to provide the employees with the **necessary technology** to work remotely.
- It can be **difficult** to **monitor working hours** and the **productivity** of employees who work remotely.
- Remote working can lead to **workers feeling isolated** and **out of touch with business goals**. The lack of social interaction can also **negatively affect motivation**.

It should also be appreciated that remote working on a permanent basis is not possible if the job requires **direct contact with customers**.

Essential Knowledge Checklist

*Questions you should now be able to answer on **organisational structures**:*

1. Define the following terms: a) organisational structure b) hierarchical organisational structure c) flat organisational structure d) centralised organisational structure e) decentralised organisational structure f) communication g) efficiency h) motivation i) barriers to communication j) jargon k) part-time hours l) full-time hours m) flexible working hours n) permanent contracts o) temporary contracts p) freelance contracts q) remote working.

2. Explain the difference between a hierarchical and a flat organisational structure.

3. Explain the difference between a centralised and a decentralised structure.

4. Explain **one** potential advantage of each of the following types of organisational structure: a) hierarchical b) flat c) centralised d) decentralised.

5. Explain **one** potential disadvantage of each of the following types of organisational structure: a) hierarchical b) flat c) centralised d) decentralised.

6. Explain **one** reason why each of the following organisational structures might be appropriate for a business: a) hierarchical b) flat c) centralised d) decentralised.

7. Explain **one** reason why effective communication is important for a business / Explain **one** benefit to a business of effective (or improved) communication.

8. Explain **one** impact on a business of each of the following: a) insufficient communication b) excessive communication.

9. Explain **one** barrier to effective communication.

10. Explain **one** reason why a business might employ people on part-time hours.

11. Explain **one** reason why a business might prefer to employ people on full-time hours as opposed to part-time hours.

12. Explain **one** benefit for a business of providing employees with the opportunity to work flexible hours.

13. Explain **one** potential drawback for a business of providing employees with the opportunity to work a) part-time hours b) full-time hours c) flexible hours.

14. Give **one** reason why a business might a) employ people on a permanent contract b) employ people on a temporary contract c) use independent contractors.

15. Explain **one** potential drawback of each of the following: a) employing people on permanent contracts b) employing people on temporary contracts c) using independent contractors.

16. Explain **one** potential benefit for a business of allowing its employees to work remotely.

17. Explain **one** potential drawback for a business of allowing its employees to work remotely.

Effective Recruitment (2.5.2)

What you need to learn

Different job roles and responsibilities:

➢ key job roles and their responsibilities: directors, senior managers, supervisors / team leaders, operational and support staff.

How businesses recruit people:

➢ documents: person specification and job description, application form, CV
➢ recruitment methods used to meet different business needs - internal and external recruitment and the advantages and drawbacks of these methods of recruitment.

Introduction

KT **Recruitment** is the process of establishing the need for a new employee, the job requirements, the type of person to fit the job, and attracting the most appropriate candidate for the job.

Different job roles and responsibilities

Key job roles and their responsibilities: directors, senior managers, supervisors / team leaders, operational and support staff

Directors

KT A **director** is one of the **most senior members** of an organisation who is elected by the shareholders each year and is responsible for making key business decisions on the shareholders' behalf. They only exist in certain types of business, mainly **incorporated** businesses, ie **limited companies**. They are mostly concerned with the **strategic** (ie medium to long-term) **direction of the business** and are responsible for:

- **setting and overseeing the achievement of medium to long-term goals** - the business's corporate and strategic objectives.

- **ensuring the company meets its statutory (legal) obligations** - for example - ensuring the company's annual reports and accounts are filed and any corporation tax due is paid on time, and the company meets its legal obligations in terms of the health, safety and welfare at work of its workers, as well as complying with environmental legislation and anti-corruption legislation.

Directors may **appoint managers to assist** them in the day to day running of the business and to make operational and tactical decisions on their behalf.

Remember, under Company Law, a private limited company need only have **one** director. In a public limited company, there has to be **two** directors. Where there is **more than one** director, the directors form the **board of directors**, which approves (or otherwise) all **long-term strategic decisions** of the company.

Senior managers

KT A **manager** is a member of staff who has authority over a number of other individuals or groups within a business and the responsibility for **planning, organising, monitoring** and **controlling the achievement** of **short to medium term goals**.

KT **Senior managers** might guide workers (operational and support staff - see below) directly, but are more likely to **direct other (less senior) managers or supervisors** who, in turn, directly manage the workers (ie operational and support staff). Typical responsibilities of senior managers include:

- Clarifying and communicating business aims and objectives and plans to achieve these (strategies) to junior managers and / or supervisors employed in the part of the business for which they are responsible.
- Directing and guiding junior managers and / or supervisors.
- Monitoring and controlling the use of resources eg through the use of budgets and approving requests for investment.
- Approving hiring and firing requests from junior managers and / or supervisors.
- Identifying training and development needs of junior managers and / or supervisors.
- Working with other senior managers to ensure shared goals and to formulate and agree strategy (ie plans to achieve the business's aims and objectives).
- Reporting on the performance of their part of the business - in relation to key performance indicators - to the board of directors.

Supervisors and team leaders

KT A **supervisor** is a member of staff who has authority over one or several individuals or group of individuals within an organisation and is responsible for their performance on a day to day basis. It is the **most junior managerial position** within an organisation. It is their job to ensure that individuals under their supervision carry out work related tasks according to the **standards laid down** on a day to day basis. Supervisors should, therefore, have sufficient knowledge and experience in the tasks these individuals have to undertake in order to be able to **advise** and **instruct them** appropriately, and **resolve task related problems** as they arise.

Supervisors generally have the power to decide **how tasks should be divided** amongst a group, and to **change the roles of group members**, but do **not** generally have the power to **hire or fire** employees, or to **promote** them. A supervisor usually recommends such action to the next level of management.

KT A **team leader** is a member of staff who has authority over a group of individuals within an organisation, who are required to work together cohesively in order to achieve a common (often) short-term goal. The team leader is responsible for **ensuring team goals are met**. One of the most important aspects of their role is to **encourage and maintain group cohesion (effective teamwork)**. Team leaders may, therefore, decide **how tasks should be allocated** amongst team members, taking into account the individual strengths of members of their team (knowledge, ability, past experience, etc). They may also be involved in the **selection and appointment of team members** to ensure the right blend of skills and personal qualities to maintain team effectiveness. They may **assign specific targets** for individual members to achieve and **evaluate individual's performance against the targets** set.

Operational and support staff

KT **Operational staff** are the people who make a business's products, or provide its service to customers. It is their responsibility to ensure the product is made (or service is provided) **according to the standards laid down and expected** by the business and its customers. **KT** **Support staff** are the group of people who work for a business to support the people who are involved in the business's main activity.

> *In a school, for example:*
>
> The **operational staff** are the **teachers**, but a wide range of **support staff** are required to ensure the school runs efficiently. These include: **office admin** staff; **learning support** staff (teaching assistants); **pupil support** staff - staff responsible for the welfare of pupils during breaks and lunchtime, or who **assist pupils with social, emotional or behavioural difficulties**, and staff who provide careers advice; **specialist and technical staff** such as science, CDT and ICT technicians and managers, librarians.

How businesses recruit people

Documents: person specification and job description, application form, CV

As part of its recruitment process a business will draw up a **job description** and a **person specification** and may also produce and ask candidates to complete **a standard application form** when applying for a job, or ask candidates to submit a **CV** (curriculum vitae). Each of these documents is briefly described below.

KT A **person specification** is a detailed description of the knowledge, skills, experience, qualifications, physical characteristics and type of personality required to carry out a job. These requirements are often ranked as 'essential' or 'desirable'. Drawing up the person specification is **the most important stage** of the recruitment process. It is against this document that candidate's applications are checked and those with the closest 'match' are invited for further assessment.

© Claire Baker - APT Initiatives Ltd, 2018
© Claire Baker - APT Initiatives Ltd, 2018

KT A **job description** is a broad statement of the key features of a job including title, purpose, tasks, targets, responsibilities and relationship to others.

KT A **standard application form (SAF)** typically contains the following sections which candidates are required to complete: contact details, date of birth, education / qualifications, employment history, any training courses attended; a statement containing additional evidence in support of the application - for example - referring to personal interests and hobbies; contact details of referees. Businesses might prefer candidates to complete an SAF rather than a CV as it makes comparison of candidates easier and shows their ability to write neatly and accurately (if not word-processed).

KT A **CV** (which stands for curriculum vitae) is a document in support of a job application which a candidate produces. It typically includes a statement summarising personal qualities, key positions held and achievements to date, and then expansion of some of these points and additional details as follows: key achievements, employment history, education / qualifications, personal interests, contact details of referees.

Recruitment methods used to meet different business needs - internal and external recruitment, including advantages and disadvantages

Overview

Once the type of person required to fill a post has been identified, a business needs to decide whether the job can be filled from inside (**internal recruitment**) or from outside (**external recruitment**) the business. Whether **internal** or **external** recruitment is chosen will very much depend upon the following:

- whether or not there are staff of the **calibre required** for the post **internally**.
- whether or not the business wants to **bring in fresh ideas** and **experience**.
- the **budget** available – external recruitment generally tends to be more expensive.
- the effect the decision will have on the **morale and motivation of existing staff**.

Internal recruitment

KT **Internal recruitment** involves attracting applicants for a post from *within* the business. **Advantages** of internal (over external) recruitment include the following:

- There is **less risk of appointing the 'wrong' person for the job**. This is because internal candidates - their strengths and weaknesses - are known to the business, and so it is easier to make an accurate assessment about their suitability for a post.

- The recruitment process is likely to be **faster** than with external recruitment. This is because there are usually fewer applicants to screen than if the job is advertised externally. Internal candidates are also already known to the business, and so less time is likely to be needed to test / assess a candidate's suitability for a post.

- Recruiting from inside the business is likely to be **less expensive** than recruiting from outside the business. This is because it avoids the cost of advertising and contacting applicants, and there are usually fewer applicants to screen.

- An employee recruited from inside the business is likely to require a much **shorter induction period** than an external candidate. This is because an internal employee is already familiar with the firm, its activities and people who work there. Therefore, they are likely to settle into their new post more quickly and with less disruption.

- A policy of recruiting internally could help to **attract**, **retain and motivate staff**. This is because if there is a chance of promotion then this may encourage staff to stay and work hard, thereby helping to maximise productivity and minimise labour turnover and the associated costs.

Disadvantages associated with internal recruitment include the following:

- There is **limited choice of applicants** – if not used in conjunction with external.

- There is **lost opportunity to bring in a fresh perspective** on the business and how it operates - for example - new cost saving / money making ideas.

- It **creates a vacancy elsewhere in the business** – if it involves internal promotion.

- It can **cause resentment** and **negatively affect the morale and motivation of internal candidates** not selected for the post.

- It can be **difficult** for an employee promoted internally to **manage people he / she previously worked alongside**.

- Internal candidates might require **training and development** to provide them with the necessary skills and experience to fulfil a post.

External recruitment

KT **External recruitment** involves attracting applicants for a post from *outside* the business. The advantages and disadvantages of external recruitment are largely the **reverse** of those listed under advantages and disadvantages of internal recruitment.

With external recruitment:

- There is **greater choice of applicants**.

- It **brings in a fresh perspective** on the business and how it operates. This, in itself, can be motivating for others who have worked there for several years.

- It may **bring in expertise from other firms**, which may be especially useful if the organisation wishes to make changes to existing practices.

- It **does not create a vacancy elsewhere** in the business.

- There are **potentially lower training costs** than those involved in promoting an internal candidate. This is because with a greater choice of applicants, the business may be more likely to find someone with the required skills and experience.

The **disadvantages**, which are essentially the reverse of the advantages of internal recruitment, include the following:

- There is **greater risk of employing the 'wrong' person for the job** than with internal recruitment. This is because the candidate does not have a proven track record with the business. Therefore, it is harder to accurately assess their suitability for the job.

- The recruitment process is likely to **take longer** than with internal recruitment. This is because there are usually more applicants to screen than if the job were advertised internally and the external candidate is not already known to the business. Therefore, more time is likely to be needed to test / assess the candidate's suitability for a post.

- External recruitment is likely to be **more expensive** than recruiting from inside the business. This is because it often involves advertising costs and usually additional internal costs - with more applicants to screen and contact.

- An employee recruited from outside the business is likely to require a **longer induction period** than an internal candidate. This is because they will be unfamiliar with the firm, its activities and people. Therefore, they are likely to require more information to be given to them when they join the business in order to settle in, and it will take longer for them to be fully productive.

- A new recruit appointed from outside the business might **not be readily accepted by others / may encounter problems in gaining the support of existing staff**, especially if an existing, internal employee had hoped to get the job. This is because existing staff may feel disgruntled and resentful that a new member of staff has been appointed from outside the business instead of them.

Essential Knowledge Checklist

Questions you should now be able to answer on **effective recruitment**:

1. Define the following terms: a) recruitment b) directors c) managers d) senior managers e) supervisors f) team leaders g) operational staff h) support staff i) person specification j) job description k) application form l) CV m) internal recruitment n) external recruitment.
2. Give **one** responsibility of each of the following job roles: a) directors b) senior managers c) supervisors d) team leaders e) operational staff f) support staff.
3. Give **one** document used in the recruitment process.
4. Explain **one** advantage of: a) internal recruitment / recruiting from inside the business; b) external recruitment / recruiting from outside the business.
5. Explain **one** disadvantage of: a) internal recruitment / recruiting from inside the business; b) external recruitment / recruiting from outside the business.

Effective Training and Development (2.5.3)

What you need to learn

How businesses train and develop employees:

➤ different ways of training and developing employees: formal and informal training, self-learning, ongoing training for all employees, including the advantages and disadvantages of these types of training; use and importance of target setting and performance reviews / the appraisal process - to identify training needs (such as the ability to use new technology) and methods of motivating individuals and / or retaining them within the business.

Why businesses train and develop employees:

➤ improved quality and customer service, improved productivity and motivation - the link between training, motivation and retention
➤ retraining to use new technology, such as a new machine or computer system.

Introduction

KT **Training** is the process of developing the knowledge, skills and attitudes required to competently and confidently carry out a job. It is usually associated with fulfilling an **immediate job role**.

KT **Development** is the process of building upon employees' existing knowledge, skills and attitudes to enable them to cope with changes to existing job roles and / or fulfil new job roles likely to be required or to become available in **the future**.

How businesses train and develop employees

Different ways of training

Formal training

KT **Formal training** is where the desired learning outcomes (in terms of knowledge, skills and attitudes) are taught in a very **structured** manner, with all content and learning materials, including estimated timings for delivery, being **planned** and **prepared prior** to the training taking place. This may involve sending the employee away to attend **a course** related to their work, at a college of further or higher education, for example. It can, however, take place in **specialist training areas** or establishments **within** the business. There are a variety of methods that can be used, including **lectures**, **demonstrations**, **simulations** and **role play**.

Advantages of formal (in comparison to informal) training include the fact that:

- Training is usually **provided by specialists** and so is likely to be of high quality.
- There is **greater control** over the learning experience of the trainee.
- If the training takes place outside the workplace, workplace **distractions** are avoided. Therefore, the trainee may find it **easier to concentrate** and, therefore, they may **learn more quickly**.

Disadvantages include the fact that:

- This sort of training is generally **very expensive** in comparison to informal training.
- If it takes place outside the workplace the trainee is **removed from 'production'**, which **lowers productivity**.

Informal training

KT **Informal training** is where the desired learning outcomes (in terms of knowledge, skills and attitudes) are learnt in a **relaxed, flexible** manner. It is **less planned and structured** (than formal training).

The most well-known method of informal training is learning from **experience on the job**. When an employee first joins a workplace, this may simply involve an experienced employee showing the trainee exactly what to do - with both trainee and trainer usually working alongside one another, until the new recruit is considered competent enough to work without guidance / supervision.

Informal training may also involve **KT** **coaching** - where an expert demonstrates and guides the worker through the job, and / or **KT** **mentoring** - where the trainee actually carries out the job but discusses any problems and solutions with their mentor as required. **Mentoring** is usually only used where the trainee already has **some experience** in the job.

In terms of **advantages** (in comparison to formal training):

- Informal training is **job specific, directly linked to the firm's needs**, relatively **easy to organise, adaptable** and **inexpensive**.

In terms of **disadvantages** and / or limitations:

- There is a **loss in productivity** whilst the new recruit settles in. This is because an experienced employee is often used to train a new employee.
- The trainer also needs to be selected very carefully - to **ensure 'bad practice' isn't passed on**.
- It may also be difficult to train an employee properly 'on the job' when there are **sudden peaks in orders / demand**.

Self-learning

KT **Self-learning** is learning undertaken by oneself, without a teacher or instructor. In a work situation this would include **acquiring knowledge by trial and error whilst working** on a job. In terms of **advantages**, the trainee might feel **less pressure** to get things right first time, than with other methods of training. **However**, the trainee might **not find it easy to access help** if and when difficulties are encountered.

Ongoing training for all employees

KT **Ongoing training** is training which continues after an employee has attained the knowledge, skills and attitudes required to carry out a job to the standards expected by the business. Ongoing training is important for the following reasons:

- To ensure **key things are not forgotten** and **best practice and high standards are maintained**, in order to **maximise quality and productivity**.

- To ensure a business **keeps up to date with changes** in the business environment, such as changes in **technology, legislation, consumer needs and expectations** and / or **competitor activities**. Keeping up to date with such changes could be crucial in **maintaining a competitive edge** and, thus, in **maximising sales** and **market share**.

- To enable employees to take up **internal promotion opportunities**. Offering employees ongoing training when they join a business, which enables them to advance their career, can help to **attract and retain good staff** and, thereby, **reduce recruitment and labour turnover** and the **associated costs**.

Use and importance of target setting and performance reviews / the appraisal process

Target setting

KT **Target setting**, in a training and development context, involves setting goals for individual employees (or units / sections / departments) within a business to achieve. These should ideally be derived from the overall aims and objectives of the business. They should also be SMART, that is:

- **Specific** – state exactly what it relates to eg Sales? Profit?
- **Measurable** – provide a yardstick against which performance can be measured eg increase output by 10%.
- **Agreed** by all those directly involved – people are more likely to understand the objective and more likely to be motivated to achieve it.
- **Realistic** – if a target is perceived to be unachievable, then this will only serve to demotivate rather than motivate.
- **Timescaled** – ie state by when the target must be achieved. This is important to provide impetus and allow measurement to take place.

© Claire Baker - APT Initiatives Ltd, 2018

© Claire Baker - APT Initiatives Ltd, 2018

Setting employees individual targets to achieve can be highly **beneficial** for a business:

- It may result in employees becoming **more motivated** at work and, thus, **more productive,** and so the business will benefit from **lower unit costs.**
- It can help a business **control** the activities of its workers, possibly with **less supervision** and, therefore, **lower costs.**

This is because individual targets provide **something specific to work towards** and a **means of measuring individual performance.** Achieving such targets may also be a way of **securing a reward,** or **avoiding sanctions** for failing to do so. This will help employees to **stay focused on work related matters** and **avoid being distracted.** It may, ultimately, ensure **overall business aims and objectives are met.** Indeed, individual targets can be useful in **aligning an employee's personal goals with business goals** – as individual targets can be linked to a business's overall aims and objectives.

Performance reviews / The appraisal process

KT **Performance reviews** are where an employee's line manager (or in some cases peers, though this is not so common) takes on the role of an appraiser and meets with an employee (the appraisee) to discuss their (the employee's) performance over a given period of time (usually a year), against pre-set criteria. These criteria may concern:

- volume or quality of work.
- attendance and punctuality.
- appearance and hygiene (important in certain professions eg catering and medical).
- personal qualities such as reliability, flexibility, willingness to take responsibility and contribution to teamwork.

It also typically involves the line manger discussing and agreeing **future targets** with the employee, eg in terms of volume, value, time, cost, career progression and training needs of the employee.

Appraisal should be a **'two-way' process.** The employee (appraisee) should be given the chance to comment on aspects relating to his / her performance, strengths and weaknesses, future targets, career progression and training needs, followed by the appraiser's opinions on each of these, and an agreement reached wherever possible.

If carried out effectively, **for the employee,** performance reviews / the appraisal process can help to satisfy a number of **physical and psychological needs**, as follows:

- **Pay may increase** as a result of **meeting or exceeding targets** set in previous appraisals. This can help to satisfy employee's **basic needs** - providing the means to pay for food and accommodation etc and may make employees feel **more secure** - as it increases their ability to pay for food, bills etc in the future.

- Employees are given **support and guidance**, with **training** being arranged where required - in order to **build on strengths, overcome weaknesses** and **achieve their career aspirations.** This 'open' communication can help to satisfy employees' **social needs** (ie the need for personal interaction), make employees **feel valued,** as well as help to **eliminate any feelings of anxiety,** which can make employees feel **safe / more secure.**

- Employees may be given **positive, verbal feedback** (not just pay) for a job well done. This can make them feel **appreciated and valued** and, ultimately, help them to **feel good about themselves,** which can increase their **self-esteem.**

- Employees may be given **extra responsibilities or recognition** of capability through **promotion.** This can help them to feel more **fulfilled.**

For a business, conducting performance reviews / undertaking appraisals may:

- **increase employee motivation** and, thus, **improve employee performance / increase productivity.** This is because performance reviews provide a mechanism for managers to give employees feedback on their performance and any areas for improvement.

- help to **identify training and development needs.** This will ensure employees are able to carry out their job to the required standard and will, in turn, help to **maximise their productivity.**

- help to **retain employees** and, thus, **reduce labour turnover and associated costs.** This is because performance reviews provide the opportunity for employees to air any grievances / concerns / frustrations and for appropriate action to be taken (wherever possible) to resolve these concerns.

- reduce the **chance of conflict** arising in the workplace, which can negatively affect productivity. This is because performance reviews provide an opportunity to **clarify employees' roles / responsibilities.**

- **eliminate duplication of effort,** for example, where one person is working on a task which someone else is also working on, or has already completed, which wastes time and resources. This is also because performance reviews provide an opportunity to **clarify employees' roles / responsibilities.**

- aid **coordination and control.** This is also because performance reviews provide the opportunity to **clarify the business's aims and objectives** with individual employees, which can help to ensure **everyone works towards a common goal.**

To conclude, through the process of appraisal, a business is able to make better plans and provision for its employees, and can exert considerable influence on the way they develop. It helps to individualise monetary rewards, training and promotional plans for each employee, which can be geared towards achieving business aims and objectives.

Why businesses train and develop employees

The link between training, motivation and retention

Employees are likely to be **more satisfied and better-motivated** when businesses invest in training them. They are, therefore, less **likely to leave** to find work elsewhere. This is because:

- Training ensures employees competently and confidently carry out their job, which, in turn, can help to **minimise feelings of anxiety** and make them feel **more secure**.

- Employees may feel management **value them**, as they are willing to invest time and money in training and developing them. This can increase employees' **self-esteem**.

- Employees may be able to **undertake more interesting / challenging work**, which enables them to fully exploit their abilities. This can make employees feel **more fulfilled**. It also improves employees' job prospects / chances of promotion.

By helping to **maximise staff retention**, this will **minimise labour turnover** and **associated costs** - for example - the cost of advertising a post, contacting and interviewing potential applicants, and of inducting and training new employees.

A reputation for training can also help to **attract (as well as retain) good quality staff** thereby aiding the recruitment process. Training can also help to **create a more flexible workforce**. This is because workers are able to do a wider range of jobs and are better able to cope with changes affecting jobs in the future.

It should be appreciated, however, that the main aim of training is to develop the knowledge, skills and attitudes required to **competently** and **confidently** carry out a job / perform a particular task to the **standard required**, which is vital for the following reasons:

- To ensure products / services **meet customer expectations** and, thus, **minimise costs** arising from poor quality work / customer service, for example: the cost of **additional materials and labour hours** arising from **re-working** poor quality goods; the cost of dealing with **customer complaints** from dissatisfied customers; **lost sales** arising from **lack of repeat business** or **poor word of mouth**.

- To **maximise productivity** ie the output that can be achieved per employee within a certain time. This will **minimise unit labour costs** and, thus, **maximise profitability**.

- To reduce the number of **supervisors** required, and thus the **cost of supervision**. This is because trained staff are likely to be **more productive**, ie quicker at their job and make **fewer mistakes**.

- To minimise the **chance of accidents** occurring and, thus, the **costs from fines** incurred for **breaches in health and safety legislation**, and / or **lost sales** arising from **negative publicity**.

With regard to the final bullet point above, it should be remembered (from Theme 1) that training is also **a legal requirement**. Employers have a legal responsibility to provide adequate health and safety training and employees have a legal responsibility to ensure they carry out their duties in accordance with any health and safety training provided. Failure to provide adequate health and safety training is contrary to health and safety legislation and could result in **fines** or **costs** from claims for compensation.

To conclude, investment in training is essential in **maximising a business's profits and profitability** - by not only helping to ensure the business meets customer needs and expectations which is crucial in **maximising sales**, but also by **maximising efficiency** and **minimising costs**.

Retraining to use new technology

Employees may have to be retrained as a result of **new technology** being introduced into the workplace. This will ensure that they are competently and confidently able to use the new technology, such as a new machine or computer system.

Essential Knowledge Checklist

*Questions you should now be able to answer on **effective training and development**:*

1. Define the following terms: a) training b) formal training c) informal training d) self-learning e) ongoing training for all employees f) target setting e) performance reviews / appraisal.
2. You should also be able to define: a) coaching b) mentoring.
3. Give **one** method of each of the following: a) formal training b) informal training.
4. Give **one** advantage of each of the following ways of training: a) formal training b) informal training c) self-learning.
5. Give **one** disadvantage of each of the following ways of training: a) formal training b) informal training c) self-learning.
6. Explain **one** reason why a business might invest in ongoing training for all employees.
7. Explain **one** benefit for a business of setting employees individual targets to achieve.
8. Explain **one** benefit for a business of having performance reviews with its employees.
9. Explain **one** reason why businesses train and develop employees.
10. Discuss the impact of poor training on a business.

© Claire Baker - APT Initiatives Ltd, 2018

© Claire Baker - APT Initiatives Ltd, 2018

Motivation (2.5.4)

What you need to learn

The importance of motivation in the workplace:

➢ attracting employees, retaining employees (reducing staff turnover), productivity.

How businesses motivate employees:

➢ financial methods: remuneration, bonus, commission, promotion, fringe benefits
➢ non-financial methods: job rotation, job enrichment, autonomy.

Introduction

KT Motivation is not just about persuading a person to do a particular job but persuading them to do it well. If management can do this successfully, then the business can benefit in a number of ways.

The importance of motivation in the workplace

Overview

People have **needs** or **goals** that motivate them to work hard in a particular job. If these are **not satisfied** then employees may become **frustrated**, resulting in any of the following symptoms:

- **lateness, absence, sickness** and / or **poor staff retention / high labour turnover.**
- **poor quality** work and / or **low output** of work (**low productivity**).
- unwillingness to take **responsibility**.
- **quarrels** with colleagues and / or disputes with management.
- **accidents**.
- **damage** to equipment or property.

All of the above can lead to **increased costs, lost sales** and **reduced profits**, due to **waste** or **inefficiency**.

In contrast, when employees are highly motivated they are likely to be **more productive** resulting in **high output** per worker and thus **low labour cost per unit**. They are also likely to produce **higher quality** work, which will result in **high customer satisfaction** and, thus, repeat business, as well as new business from recommendations. Employees are also **less likely to leave** to find work elsewhere, resulting in **high retention rates** and, thus, **low labour turnover** and **associated costs**.

Attracting employees

A well-motivated workforce can generate a **positive image** about the business which can help to **attract good staff**, thereby making it **easier** and **cheaper** to secure the number of staff required to achieve business aims and objectives.

Retaining employees / Reducing staff turnover

A well-motivated workforce is important in helping to **retain good staff** and, thus, in **minimising labour turnover and the associated costs**. These include: the cost of advertising a post, contacting and interviewing potential applicants and inducting and training new employees.

Productivity

A well-motivated workforce contributes significantly to **maximising productivity / output per employee**. This is because motivated employees are likely to take **more of an interest** in their job, and so they are more likely to:

- **maximise effort** resulting in **greater output**.
- **make fewer mistakes**, thereby **minimising time wasted correcting errors**. A well-motivated workforce is, in fact, important in **ensuring high product / service quality**, which, besides helping to maximise productivity is important in **minimising costs** - from reworking poor quality goods, as well as in **maximising sales** - from repeat business and new business from positive word of mouth / recommendations.
- **make the effort to get to work** and **to get to work on time**, thereby **minimising time lost** as a result of **lateness** and / or **absenteeism**, as well as **minimising costs** - of sick pay and management time spent organising cover.

Any increase in productivity will **reduce unit costs (labour costs per unit)**, which will **increase profits** and / or enable the business to be **more competitive on price**, which could be crucial in **maximising sales and market share**.

How businesses motivate employees

Financial methods

Introduction

Financial methods of motivation are methods of motivation that have a monetary value. With such methods of motivation, there is scope for students to be asked calculation questions. Some examples are, therefore, provided below.

© Claire Baker - APT Initiatives Ltd, 2018
© Claire Baker - APT Initiatives Ltd, 2018

Remuneration

KT **Remuneration** is a general term covering any type of money paid for work undertaken. People are either paid according to the **time** they spend at work ie **KT** **time-based pay**, or they are paid according to the quantity and / or quality of the work they produce ie **KT** **merit-based pay** (or payment by results).

Time-based pay includes wages and salaries. **KT** **Wages** are monies earned by employees in return for their labour or services which are paid on an hourly, daily, or weekly basis. A **KT** **salary** is an annual amount paid to employees (normally to supervisory, clerical and managerial workers) for work undertaken. It is paid monthly, in 12 equal instalments, and is not related to output, profits or hours of work, although rates are usually fixed in relation to a standard number of hours worked per week, which would be written into an employee's contract of employment.

Example (wages): A business pays its Office Administrator £15 per hour. If the Office Administrator works 39 hours a week, their weekly gross pay (ie weekly wage before any deductions for tax and national insurance) would be: 39 x £15 = **£585**.

Example (salary): The annual salary paid to a Production Manager is £32,520. The Production Manager's monthly gross pay (ie before any deductions for tax and national insurance) would be calculated as follows: £32,520 / 12 = **£2,710**.

Merit-based pay includes piece-rate pay and performance-related pay. **KT** **Piece-rate pay** is where workers are paid for each quality item produced. **KT** **Performance-related pay** is where part of an employee's pay is linked to the achievement of pre-defined (and agreed) targets. **Merit-based pay** may also include **commission** or a **bonus** for achieving certain targets. Commission and bonuses are discussed later below.

Example (piece-rate pay): A manufacturing firm pays each of its production staff £3.50 per item produced. If a production worker produces 130 items during one week, the amount they would receive for this work would be: £3.50 x 130 = **£455**.

Bonus

KT A **bonus** is a sum of money awarded to an employee (or employees) as a one-off payment to recognise their contribution - to sales or profits for example, or for achieving pre-determined targets. Alternatively, bonuses may be given that are not linked to individual or business performance, but simply issued to boost employees' pay at certain times of the year, for example, at Christmas.

Example (bonus): A retailer pays its sales assistants an annual salary of £14,670. It also decided to pay each of its sales assistants an additional annual bonus last year worth 8% of their annual salary. In monetary terms, each sales assistant would have received the following bonus: £14,670 x 0.08 = **£1,173.60**.

Bonuses are more likely to **increase motivation** and **improve performance**, when they are linked to the achievement of **specific targets**. As previously explained, the setting of targets on their own can be motivating – encourage employees to **work hard / harder** and providing a **sense of achievement** once reached. The subsequent **reward** for the achievement of these targets in the form of a bonus provides **recognition of effort**, which can boost **people's self-esteem / self-worth** or, in simple terms, make them feel good about themselves and what they have achieved.

Commission

KT **Commission** is a fee paid to an employee (or agent) for services performed, which varies according to their output. It is common to sales positions and is usually a percentage of the total amount received in a sales transaction. It is a form of **performance-related pay** and can incentivise staff to work hard - as **the more leads converted into sales**, **the more money they earn**.

Example (commission): A business pays its sales staff a basic salary plus 15% of the selling price of every unit sold. If a member of its sales staff sold 50 units at £72 per unit, then the amount of commission earned would be: (£72 x 0.15) x 50 = **£540**.

Promotion

KT **Promotion**, in the context of human resources, is the appointment of an employee to a higher position within an organisation, which usually brings additional responsibilities and higher pay. It can be an important factor in helping to motivate employees. This is because it can provide employees with:

- **higher pay**, which is important in the satisfaction of people's **basic** needs (ie in order to pay for essential items such as food, clothes, accommodation, etc).
- a **sense of achievement**, which can help to increase people's **self-esteem** / make them feel good about themselves.
- higher **status**, which can also help to increase people's **self-esteem**.
- greater **responsibility**, which provides scope for employees to undertake more challenging tasks and, thus, to utilise more of their abilities, which can make them feel **more fulfilled**.

Opportunities for promotion can also **increase the retention of staff**. This is because such opportunities may encourage staff to **stay** and **work hard** to secure promotion.

Fringe benefits

KT **Fringe benefits** are any benefit provided to employees in addition to their basic pay. They can be financial or non-financial, although the majority do have a **financial** value. They might include private health insurance, a company car, gym membership, and discounts on a firm's products or services.

© Claire Baker - APT Initiatives Ltd, 2018

Fringe benefits may help to **attract and retain staff**. This is because employees may prefer some benefits rather than pay, such as private medical insurance, which reduces the time people have to wait for treatment.

Fringe benefits may also be a **cheaper method of motivation** to implement than **higher pay**. This is because the business has to pay 'secondary' Class 1 National Insurance Contributions (NICs) on all employees' earnings above a certain weekly threshold.

Non-financial methods

Job rotation

KT **Job rotation** involves providing employees with job variety by changing their job or tasks at various intervals. For example, it may include moving an employee from one part of a production line to carry out a different task, or to a new department (eg from finance to personnel), to complete tasks requiring skills common to both.

Job rotation may help to **retain employees** and, thus, **minimise labour turnover** and the associated costs. This is because it can make an employee's job **more interesting** and, thus, it can **increase job satisfaction** and **make employees less likely to leave** to find more interesting work elsewhere. Making a job more interesting can also increase **employee motivation** which can, in turn, **increase productivity**.

Job rotation may also **increase flexibility** within the business and help to **maximise productivity**. This is because it enables employees to carry out a **wider range of tasks** and, as a result, employees are more able to **cover for absent colleagues.**

On the other hand, job rotation could result in a **fall in productivity**. This is because employees no longer **specialise** in doing one particular job / task, where they are likely to build up **expertise** and so complete the job **quickly** and / or with **fewer errors**. Implementing job rotation can also lead to **claims for additional pay**.

Job enrichment

KT **Job enrichment** involves giving employees more challenging tasks and / or greater responsibility. It provides employees with opportunities to utilise more of their skills / demonstrate more of their abilities, thereby **enriching** (ie improving the quality or value of) the job they do.

Job enrichment may result in employees being **more satisfied** and **motivated at work**. This is because it involves giving employees **more meaningful, interesting work** and may also provide the opportunity for staff to **utilise more of their skills** and so they may feel **more fulfilled**. This can help to **retain staff** and, thus, **minimise labour turnover** and the associated costs.

There are, however, some **potential drawbacks**, as follows:

- Some **initial training** may be required - to ensure workers are able to carry out new tasks / responsibilities to the standard required, and this **incurs costs**.
- It may also **increase wages / salary costs**. This is because employees (and / or their representatives) may argue that increased responsibility requires additional pay. This could make the business **less competitive on price**.
- Like job rotation, it could also result in a **drop in productivity**. This is because the employee no longer **specialises** in a **narrow range of tasks**, where they are likely to build up **expertise** and so complete the job **quickly** and / or with **fewer errors**.

Autonomy

The word '**autonomy**' means, self-government, independence and freedom. In a work situation, **KT** **autonomy** means giving staff freedom to make decisions over work-related issues. This can make employees **more motivated** because:

- It may make staff feel **more trusted** and **valued**, which can help to increase people's **self-esteem** / make them feel good about themselves.
- It may provide staff with the opportunity to **use more of their potential**, which can help them to feel **more fulfilled**.
- Staff may feel **less stressed** – as there should be **less supervision** and **interference** in decision making.

As with other methods of motivation, employees may, therefore be:

- **more productive**, thereby reducing labour cost per unit.
- **less likely to be absent**, thereby keeping sick pay to a minimum and helping to maximise productivity.
- **less likely to leave** to work elsewhere, thereby reducing labour turnover and associated costs.

There are also **additional potential benefits** of giving staff autonomy, as follows:

- **Managers** are **freed up** to **concentrate on planning and organisational development** rather than supervision.
- The business may need **fewer managers / supervisors**, thereby benefiting from **lower costs**. This is because employees are given the freedom to make decisions over aspects of their work without having to check with a higher authority.
- It may result in potentially **better quality decisions** being made – as decisions should be made by those most suited to make them.
- The business may benefit from **faster decision making** and, thus **faster response to change**. This is because employees do not have to await (as many) decisions from managers.

© Claire Baker - APT Initiatives Ltd, 2018
© Claire Baker - APT Initiatives Ltd, 2018

However, giving staff more autonomy over work related issues requires the following:

- **a high degree of trust** – Workers should be able to carry out their jobs without constant checking from management, but some managers may find it difficult to delegate power – for fear of loss of control or the belief that employees below them in the hierarchy (subordinates) are not able to make appropriate decisions.

- **employees to feel confident** in their own abilities. Some employees may not be able or willing to take on the additional responsibility for decision making.

Training may, therefore, be essential to encourage and enable employees to take on additional responsibility for decision making, as well as to change management attitudes where necessary – to encourage them to delegate and empower employees, without fear of loss of control. Careful **recruitment and selection** would also be required to ensure individuals are selected that fit in with a more 'empowered' organisational culture, ie responsible, self-motivated, and trustworthy individuals. One other **potential drawback** is that employees might demand **more pay** for the additional responsibility.

Essential Knowledge Checklist

Questions you should now be able to answer on **motivation**:

1. Define the following terms: a) motivation b) remuneration c) bonus d) commission e) promotion f) fringe benefits g) job rotation h) job enrichment i) autonomy.
2. You should also be able to define the following: a) time-based pay b) merit-based pay c) wages d) salaries e) piece-rate pay f) performance-related pay.
3. Explain **one** reason why motivation is important in the workplace / Explain **one** benefit for a business of a well-motivated workforce / improved worker motivation.
4. Discuss the effect on a business of a poorly motivated workforce.
5. Give **one** example of a financial method of motivation.
6. Calculate the pay, bonus or commission received by an employee in a given situation.
7. Explain **one** way in which providing opportunities for promotion can benefit a business.
8. Give **one** example of a fringe benefit.
9. Explain **one** reason why a business might provide employees with fringe benefits.
10. Give **one** example of a non-financial method of motivation.
11. Explain **one** benefit for a business of each of the following methods of motivation: a) job rotation b) job enrichment c) giving staff autonomy.
12. Explain **one** potential drawback for a business of each of the following methods of motivation: a) job rotation b) job enrichment c) giving staff autonomy.

© Claire Baker - APT Initiatives Ltd, 2018

INDEX

above the line methods of promotion 46
advertising
    definition of 46
    to different market segments (through
    newspaper, magazine, radio, TV, poster) 46-47
    benefits and drawbacks of 47
aesthetics - as part of the design mix 34,35
appraisal - see performance reviews
assets 12
attitudes (as a barrier to communication) 107-8
automation
    definition and examples of 66-67
    impact of 68-70
autonomy
    definition, benefits and drawbacks of 134-35
average incomes 96
average rate of return (ARR)
    definition, calculation and use of 91
    impact of interest rates on 92
bar gate stock graph
    definition, examples and interpretation of 73
barriers to effective communication
    definition and examples of 106-108
barriers to international trade 25
batch production
    definition of 63
    advantages and disadvantages of 64-65
below the line methods of promotion 46
bonus - definition and calculation of 131-32
branding
    as a method of promotion 45
    definition, benefits and drawbacks of 49
buffer stock 72-73
business aims and objectives
    definition of 17
    why they change as businesses evolve 17-18
    how they change as businesses evolve 18-21
business calculations 87-92
business growth
    general benefits and drawbacks of 2
    methods and impact of 3-8
business location
    and globalisation 24
business operations 62-70
business ownership
    for growing businesses 8-11
    and changes in business aims & objectives 21
business performance 21,93-98
capital investment 91
centralisation 102
centralised organisational structure
    definition and appropriateness of 102
    advantages and disadvantages of 102-3
coaching 123
commission - definition and calculation of 132
communication
    definition of and stages involved in 104
    importance of 105
    impact of insufficient or excessive 105-6
    barriers to effective 106-8

competition
    as an influence on pricing strategies 43
competitive advantage
    definition of 58
    using the marketing mix to gain a 58-59
    and an integrated marketing mix 59-60
compressed working weeks 110
computer-aided-design (CAD)
    definition and use of 68
    impact of 68,70
computer-aided-manufacture (CAM)
    definition and use of 67
    impact of 68,70
consumer income
    and impact on business aims & objectives 20
cost(s)
    as part of the design mix 34,35
    as an influence on pricing strategies 42
    impact of technology on 68-70
cost of sales - definition and calculation of 87-88
credit 53,77
customer service
    definition and importance of 84-85
CV (curriculum vitae) 119
data 93, also see quantitative business data
debentures 14
decentralisation 102
decentralised organisational structure
    definition and appropriateness of 102
    advantages and disadvantages of 104 (102-3)
design mix (the) 34-35
design technology 68
development (of human resources)
    definition of 122
    reasons for investing in 127-128
direct costs 35
direct marketing 45
directors
    definition, role and responsibilities of 116-17
diseconomies of scale 2
distribution
    definition of 52
    methods of 52-55
distributors 52
dividends 15
divorce of ownership and control 10-11
e-commerce
    definition of 26
    and its use in competing internationally 26
    benefits and drawbacks of 54-55
e-newsletters 51
e-tailers
    definition, benefits and drawbacks of 54-55
economic climate
    definition of 20
    and impact on business aims and objectives 20
economies of scale 2
efficiency
    definition of 105
    impact of communication on 105-106

environmental considerations
    and influence on business activity 30
    and benefits of taking these into account 30-31
ethics / ethical considerations / business behaviour
    definition of 29
    and influence on business activity 29
    benefits of 30-31
exchange rates
    definition of 23
    and their impact on businesses that import 23
    and their impact on businesses that export 24
exports
    definition of 24
    and the impact of exchange rates 24
extension strategies
    definition and examples of 38-39
external factors
    definition of 17
    and effect on business aims & objectives 18-20
external (inorganic) growth
    definition of 6
    through mergers and takeovers 6-7
    benefits and drawbacks of 7-8
external recruitment
    definition of 120
    advantages and disadvantages of 120-21
external sources of finance
    definition and examples of 13-15
financial data
    definition, use and interpretation of 94
financial information
    use and limitations of 97-98
financial methods of motivation 130-33
fixed assets - see non-current assets
flat organisational structure
    definition of 100
    appropriateness and advantages of 101
flexible hours
    types, benefits and drawbacks of 110-11
flexitime 110
flow production
    definition of 63
    advantages and disadvantages of 65-66
foreign direct investment (FDI) 22
formal training
    definition of 122
    advantages and disadvantages of 123
freelance contracts
    definition, benefits and drawbacks of 112-13
fringe benefits 132-33
full-time hours
    definition of 110
    reasons for 110
    advantages & disadvantages of 110
function - as part of the design mix 34,35
global trade 22
globalisation
    definition of 22
    and impact on businesses 23-24
    how businesses compete internationally 26-28
goods 62
goodwill 6

gross profit
    definition and calculation of 87
    reasons for a fall in 88
    ways to increase 88
    impact of interest rates on 92
gross profit margin
    definition and calculation of 90
    reasons for a fall in 90
hierarchical organisational structure
    definition of 100
    appropriateness of 101
    advantages and disadvantages of 101
hierarchy 100
high margin, low volume pricing strategy 41
high volume, low margin pricing strategy 42
imports
    definition of 23
    and the impact of exchange rates 23
inflation
    and impact on business aims & objectives 20
    and assessing business performance 97
informal training
    definition of 123
    advantages and disadvantages of 123
information - definition of 93
innovation - definition and stages of 4
inorganic growth - see external growth
intangible assets 6
interest - calculation of 13
interest rates
    and impact on profit and ARR performance 92
    and impact on business aims & objectives 20
intermediaries (as a barrier to communication) 108
internal (organic) growth
    definition of 3
    through existing products and markets 3
    through new products 4
    through new markets 5
    benefits and drawbacks of 5
internal reasons
    why aims and objectives change 18,20-21
internal recruitment
    definition of 119
    advantages and disadvantages of 119-20
internal sources of finance
    definition and examples of 11-13
Internet
    definition of 26
    and its use in competing internationally 26
inventory - see stock
jargon (as a barrier to communication) 106
job description 119
job enrichment
    definition, benefits and drawbacks of 133-34
job production
    definition, advantages and disadvantages of 63
job rotation
    definition, benefits and drawbacks of 133
just in time (JIT) stock control
    definition, benefits and drawbacks of 74-75
lead time 69
leasing 13

legislation
    definition of 19
    and impact on business aims and objectives 19
loan capital
    definition of 13
    advantages & disadvantages / limitations of 14
location
    international 24
    of suppliers 76
logistics
    definition of 77
    impact of poor decisions in relation to 78
managers 117
manufacturing resource planning software 67
market 18
market conditions
    definition of 18
    and impact on business aims & objectives 18-19
market data
    definition, use and interpretation of 95
market segments
    definition of 43
    as an influence on pricing strategies 43
market share 95-96
market size 95-96
marketing data
    definition, use and interpretation of 95
marketing mix
    definition of 26,56
    changes in, to achieve business growth 3-5
    changes in, to compete internationally 26-28
    use of, to make business decisions 56-60
    the interrelationship of elements of 56-58
    use of, to build competitive advantage 58-59
    importance of an integrated 59-60
mass production 66
maximum stock level 73
mentoring 123
mergers
    definition, benefits and drawbacks of 6-8
merit-based pay 131
methods of distribution - see distribution
methods of finance - see sources of finance
methods of production 63-66
minimum stock level 73
motivation
    definition of 106,129
    impact of communication on 106
    and training 127
    importance of 129-30
    financial methods of 130-33
    non-financial methods of 133-35
multinationals 24
net profit
    definition and calculation of 88
    reasons to calculate 89
    reasons for a fall in 89-90
    ways to increase 90
    impact of interest rates on 92
net profit margin
    definition and calculation of 91
    reasons for a fall in 91

non-current assets 12
non-financial methods of motivation 133-35
ongoing training for all employees
    definition of 124
    reasons for 124
operational staff
    definition, role and responsibilities of 118
opportunity cost 72
organic growth - see internal growth
organisational structure
    definition and types of 100-104
other operating expenses and interest 88-90
overtrading 2
part-time hours
    definition of 109
    reasons for, advantages & disadvantages of 109
penetration pricing 44
performance reviews
    definition, use and importance of 125-26
performance-related pay 131
permanent contracts
    definition, advantages and disadvantages of 111
person specification 118
personal selling 45
piece-rate pay
    definition and calculation of 131
place (as an element of marketing mix) 52-55
    changes in, to compete internationally 28
    and its influence on other elements 58
pressure groups
    definition of 31
    and impact on the marketing mix 31
price (as an element of the marketing mix) 41-44
    changes in, to compete internationally 27
    and its influence on other elements 57
price skimming 44
pricing strategies
    definition and examples of 41-42, 44
    influences on 42-44
procurement
    definition of 75
    factors which lead to efficiency in 76-77
product (as an element of the marketing mix) 34-40
    changes in, to compete internationally 26
    and its influence on other elements 56-57
product differentiation
    definition, methods and importance of 39-40
product life cycle
    definition and phases of 36-38
    factors influencing 36
    as an influence on pricing strategies 43-44
product trials 48
production - definition of 64
production processes 63-66
productivity
    definition and calculation of 64
    impact of technology on 66-70
    impact of motivation on 130
profit 87-91
promotion (as element of the marketing mix) 45-55
    changes in, to compete internationally 27-28
    and its influence on other elements 57

promotion (in terms of human resources) 132
public limited company (plc)
    definition and key characteristics of 8-9
    advantages / benefits of 9
    disadvantages / drawbacks of 9-11
public relations 45
purchasing economies of scale 2
quality
    definition and importance of 80-81
    methods of ensuring 81-82
quality assurance 81-82
quality control 81-82
quantitative business data
    definition, use and interpretation of 93-96
recession
    and impact on business aims & objectives 20
recruitment
    definition of 116
    documents used in 118-19
    internal 119-20
    external 120-21
remote working
    definition, benefits and drawbacks of 114
remuneration 131
research and development (R&D)
    definition of 4
    stages involved in 4
retailers
    definition of 52
    benefits and drawbacks of selling through 53
retained profit
    definition of 11
    advantages & disadvantages / limitations of 12
retention (of staff)
    and the link with training 127
    and the link with motivation 130
retraining - to use new technology 128
robots / robotics
    definition and impact of 67,68,69
salary - definition and calculation of 131
sales process (the)
    definition of 83
    steps involved in 83
    key elements and impact of 84
sales promotion 45
self-learning 124
self-rostering 110
selling assets
    definition of 12
    advantages, disadvantages / limitations of 12-13
senior managers
    definition, role and responsibilities of 117
services 62
share capital
    definition of 14
    advantages & disadvantages / limitations of 15
shrinkflation 23
social media 50
sources of finance
    definition of 11
    internal 11-13
    external 13-15

span of control 101
special offers 48
sponsorship 48
standard application form (SAF) 119
stock
    definition of 71
    effective management of 71-72
    costs of holding 71-72
    reasons for holding 72
stock exchange 9
stock market flotation
    definition of 15
    advantages & disadvantages / limitations of 15
supervisors
    definition, role and responsibilities of 117
suppliers
    definition of 71
    relationships with 76-77
    and impact on a business's costs, reputation
    & customer satisfaction 78
support staff
    definition, role and responsibilities of 118
sustainability / sustainable working practices
    definition and benefits of 30-31
takeovers
    definition, benefits and drawbacks of 6-8
tangible assets 6
target setting
    definition, use and importance of 124-25
targeted advertising online 50
tariffs
    definition of 25
    as a barrier to international trade 25
team leaders
    definition, role and responsibilities of 118
technology
    definition of 19,66
    to achieve business growth 3-5
    and impact on business aims and objectives 19
    as an influence on pricing strategies 42
    and its use in promotion 50-51
    and its impact on production 66-70
    and its impact on ways of working 114
temporary contracts
    definition, advantages and disadvantages of 112
term time contracts 110
time-based pay 131
trade blocs
    definition and examples of 25
    as a barrier to international trade 25
trade-offs between
    ethics and profit 29
    the environment, sustainability and profit 30
training
    definition of 122
    different ways of 122-24
    reasons for / importance of 127-28
unemployment
    and impact on business aims & objectives 20
viral advertising via social media 50
wages - definition and calculation of 131
window dressing (in terms of business accounts) 98

© Claire Baker - APT Initiatives Ltd, 2018

© Claire Baker - APT Initiatives Ltd, 2018